THE GREEK ISLANDS
Genius Loci

View of Naxos island seen through the monumental doorway of the Archaic temple.
Thomas Hope (1769-1831)   Watercolour, 0.44x0.29 m.   Benaki Museum, Inv. No. 27375.
© 2010 Benaki Museum, Athens.

Author's acknowledgements

This series of twenty books covering the Aegean Islands is the fruit of many years of solitary dedication to a job difficult to accomplish given the extent of the subject matter and the geography involved. My belief throughout has been that only what is seen with the eyes can trustfully be written about; and to that end I have attempted to walk, ride, drive, climb, sail and swim these Islands in order to inspect everything talked about here. There will be errors in this text inevitably for which, although working in good faith, I alone am responsible. Notwithstanding, I am confident that these are the best, most clearly explanatory and most comprehensive artistic accounts currently available of this vibrant and historically dense corner of the Mediterranean.

Professor Robin Barber, author of the last, general, *Blue Guide to Greece* (based in turn on Stuart Rossiter's masterful text of the 1960s), has been very generous with support and help; and I am also particularly indebted to Charles Arnold for meticulously researched factual data on the Islands and for his support throughout this project. I could not have asked for a more saintly and helpful editor, corrector and indexer than Judy Tither. Efi Stathopoulou, Peter Cocconi, Marc René de Montalembert, Valentina Ivancich, William Forrester and Geoffrey Cox have all given invaluable help; and I owe a large debt of gratitude to John and Jay Rendall for serial hospitality and encouragement. For companionship on many journeys, I would like to thank a number of dear friends: Graziella Seferiades, Ivan Tabares, Matthew Kidd, Martin Leon, my group of Louisianan friends, and my brother Iain— all of whose different reactions to and passions for Greece have been a constant inspiration.

This work is dedicated with admiration and deep affection to Ivan de Jesus Tabares-Valencia who, though a native of the distant Andes mountains, from the start understood the profound spiritual appeal of the Aegean world.

McGILCHRIST'S GREEK ISLANDS

1. SANTORINI
& THERASIA WITH ANAPHI

Nigel McGilchrist

GENIUS LOCI PUBLICATIONS

London

McGilchrist's Greek Islands 1. Santorini & Therasia with Anaphi
First edition

Published by Genius Loci Publications
54 Eccleston Road, London W13 0RL

Nigel McGilchrist © 2010
Nigel McGilchrist has asserted his moral rights.

ISBN 978-1-907859-00-7

A CIP catalogue record of this book is available from the British Library.

The author and publisher cannot accept responsibility or liability for
information contained herein, this being in some cases difficult to verify
and subject to change.

Layout and copy-editing: Judy Tither

Cover design by Kate Buckle

Maps and plans by Nick Hill Design

Printed and bound in Great Britain by TJ International Ltd, Padstow, Cornwall

The island maps in this series are based on the cartography of
Terrain Maps
Karneadou 4, 106 75 Athens, Greece
T: +30 210 609 5759, Fx: +30 210 609 5859
terrain@terrainmaps.gr
www.terrainmaps.gr

This book is one of twenty which comprise the complete, detailed
manuscript which the author prepared for the *Blue Guide: Greece,
the Aegean Islands* (2010), and on which the *Blue Guide* was
based. Some of this text therefore appears in the *Blue Guide*.

CONTENTS

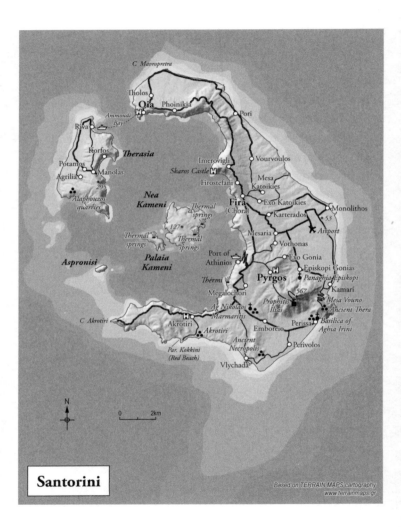

C. Mavropretra
Tholos
Oia Phoinikia
Pori
Ammoudi Bay
Riva
Korfos
Therasia
Potamos
Manolas
Agrilia
295
Alaphouzos quarries
Imerovigli
Vourvoulos
Skaros Castle
Firostefani
Mesa Kateikies
Nea Kameni
Fira (Chora)
Exo Katoikies
Monolithos
Thermal springs
Karterados
53
127
Thermal springs
Mesaria
Airport
Thermal springs
Thermal springs
Vothonas
Aspronisi
Palaia Kameni
Port of Athinios
Exo Gonia
Episkopi Gonias
Thérmi
Pyrgos
Panaghia Episkopi
Megalochori
567
Prophitis Ilias
Mesa Vouno
Ag Nikolaos Marmaritis
Ancient Thera
C. Akrotiri
Akrotiri
Emboreio
Perissa
Basilica of Aghia Irini
Kamari
Akrotiri
Ancient Necropolis
Par. Kokkini (Red Beach)
Perivolos
Vlychada

N

0   2km

Santorini

Based on TERRAIN MAPS cartography
www.terrainmaps.gr

SANTORINI

Santorini is the Mother of Volcanoes. Its caldera, seen from a boat for the first time, is a source of wonderment—something so unusual that it can only marginally be minimised by the fact that it will already be familiar from photographs. Images, though, do not do justice to the magnitude, or to the changing shapes and colours of the marine landscape as the boat cuts through the enclosed circle of islands towards the harbour, which is no more than an improvised ledge beneath a 270m, stratified cliff of lava. The view from the town above is no less extraordinary—especially at about two hours before sunset, when the vast bowl of cliffs and islands below begins to fill with a palpable light reflected on the water from the low angle of the declining sun. Santorini is an astonishing natural phenomenon; but its human history and archaeology, both prehistoric and historic, are no less astonishing. For its small size, it has one of the richest and most varied archaeological histories of any island.

The volcanic nature of the island, even before the great eruption in the 2nd millennium BC, has always shaped its history, forcing the early inhabitants into a life of maritime trade and shipping rather than agricultural production, pushing them to evolve new methods of construction to withstand their seismically active terrain, and giving them an array of brilliant volcanic earths with which to decorate their walls with paintings. Then, the eruption itself—one of the greatest, if not the greatest in human history—destroyed and buried their prospering city. But it did so in such a way that it preserved the streets and superbly decorated rooms in packed ash, until the painstaking campaigns initiated in 1967 by Spyros Marinatos first began to reveal it again to modern eyes in the excavations near the town of Akrotiri. The eruption itself was so great that the airborne blanket of volcanic powder in the stratosphere provoked a period of climatic cooling around the world; it altered the course of history in the Eastern Mediterranean; and it may be the central event at the heart of the myth of *Atlantis*, recounted by Plato. Today the same volcanic history determines the island's economy—its famous wine, the export of pumice and *pozzolana*, and the tourism it attracts which comes to gaze on this vast, toppled ruin in the sea.

Santorini today has to be taken on different terms from most of the other islands. Tourism and the incessant arrival of cruise-ships and aircraft from all corners of Europe has utterly transformed the land, the people, and the spirit of the place. But not even the artificiality and the press of humanity can diminish the island's interest or drown out the extraordinary magic of the light. It takes not much effort to find a quiet corner for contemplation of the scene: a balcony in the delightful settlement of Oia, a *plateia* in forgotten Emboreió, or a shaded taverna by the water at Akrotiri, looking across to distant Crete which nurtured the island throughout its earliest history. And for those who wish to have a glimpse of what Santorini was like a few decades back, an early morning, fifteen-minute ferry ride—which nobody except locals ever seems to take—from the harbour of Amoudi to the islet of Therasía opposite, will leave you to explore in peace a Theran landscape and villages, and to encounter the willing salutations of people whose lives have been little touched by the crowds and activity across the water.

HISTORY

Recent pottery finds at Akrotiri from the 5th millennium BC have resulted in a pushing back of the date for the first settlement of the island in Neolithic times. Although there were other smaller settlements around the island by the mid-3rd millennium, Akrotiri appears to have been the principal centre, laying the foundations for what was to become a great and cosmopolitan port in the Middle Bronze Age looking across the water to Crete. It was well-placed to profit from the copper-trading route from Cyprus, via Rhodes and Thera, to Crete and mainland Greece. The city was damaged by earthquakes and rebuilt several times before it was finally destroyed by a volcanic eruption in the late 17th century BC, which buried all human settlement and radically changed the shape of the island through the collapse of part of it under the sea. This has given rise to suggestions that it was *Metropolis*, the destroyed capital of the lost 'continent' of Atlantis. The island was subsequently uninhabited for several centuries.

Herodotus says that the island was originally called *Strongyle* ('round'); later it was referred to as *Kalliste* ('most beautiful'). In tradition it was colonised by the Phoenicians, led by Cadmus. In the 9th or 8th century

BC, Ancient *Thera*, a Dorian colony from Laconia was established on an isolated mountain site in the southeast corner of the island. It was, in true Dorian fashion, conservative in culture and in its external relations; but it was one of the first Aegean centres to adopt the Phoenician alphabet for writing the Greek language. Around 630 BC, it was forced by a protracted drought to found its own colony, Cyrene, on the north coast of Africa. In the late 6th century BC it minted its own coins, bearing the motif of two dolphins. Together with *Melos*, *Thera* avoided alliance with Athens in the 5th century BC, and at the outbreak of the Peloponnesian War in 431/430 BC, managed to escape the unpleasant fate of *Melos* at the hands of the Athenians; but it was later assessed to pay a tribute of three talents to the First Athenian League. After the Athenian defeat in 404 BC, the island returned to the sphere of Spartan influence. After 375 BC, however, it was absorbed with the other Cycladic islands into the Second Athenian League. In Hellenistic times, the island's strategic position was particularly valued by the Ptolemies, who built *Thera* and its ports up into an important, garrisoned naval base of considerable prosperity; they maintained it until the death of Ptolemy VI 'Philomator' in 145 BC. Many of the ruins visible today at Ancient *Thera* date from this period.

We hear of a Christian bishop of Thera, Dioscorus, in the mid-4th century, whose seat was probably the Basilica of St Irene at Períssa, after which the island was later named. In the early 12th century, Emperor Alexius I Comnenus founded the church of the Panaghia Episkopí on Thera. After Marco Sanudo, nephew of Doge Dandolo who had led the 4th Crusade, took the Cyclades in 1207, he ceded Santorini and Therasía to one of his followers, Giacomo Barozzi, whose descendants ruled the island from a capital at Skaros (near Imerovígli) until the Sanudo family, under Niccolo I Sanudo, desired to take it back again. He expelled the Barozzi in 1335, assuming the lordship of the island and giving the fortress of Akrotiri, in the south of the island, to the Gozzadini family. The Sanudo possessions passed to the Crispi family in 1397, and Santorini was ceded as a marriage dowry to Domenico Pisani, Duke of Crete in 1480. The island was attacked by Khaireddin Barbarossa in 1537, but came under Turkish dominion only later in 1566. In 1821 Santorini's fleet contributed considerably to the Greek War of Independence; in 1832 the island officially became part of the Greek State. A strong earthquake in July 1956 damaged or destroyed well over half the structures on the island. In recent years, several curious occurrences of negligence have brought Santorini into the news: in September 2005 a part of the newly constructed protective roof over the archaeological site at Akrotiri collapsed killing a British tourist and injuring others: the site—one of the most visited in the Aegean—closed as a result for more than four years. On 5th April 2007 the Cypriot-owned cruise-vessel, *Sea Diamond*, with 1,200 passengers aboard, ran aground east of Nea Kameni and sank 15 hours later just north of the main port of Athiniós, with the loss of two lives.

CHANGING NAMES

The island is referred to today with equal frequency as Thera and Santorini, by both Greeks and foreigners. Its ancient name is *Thera*; the name Santorini (or Santa Irene) was given currency by the Venetians in the 13th century. 'Thera' has recently been re-adopted as the official name to designate the island as part of a general policy to return to native, Greek names. Not out of any disrespect for that policy, 'Santorini' has been used in this text because it is probably more familiar to our readers. We preserve *Thera*, however, when referring to the island in antiquity. The name of the main town is Firá, although officially it is now supposed to be called Thera: on the island, it is referred to as Chora—a usage followed in the text below.

THE VOLCANIC CALDERA

The layout

The panoramic parapet just opposite the church of the Metropolis in Chora is a good vantage point for comprehending the nature of the volcanic caldera of Santorini. The caldera is the physical incarnation of the island's history. It extends below and to the west, covering an area of around eighty five square kilometres, surrounded by a broken, roughly elliptical rim. You are standing on its eastern edge at a height of c. 250m above sea level; it sweeps slowly round in two arms to north and south, and its fragmented western rim is formed by the island of Therasía across the water to the west and the small, steep rock of Asprónisi, visible just to the south of due west in the middle of the breach between the southern tip of Therasía and Santorini. These landmarks describe the contour of the vast crater which is now filled by the sea, whose surface hides water-depths of as much as 400m. In the centre of the area, two (relatively new) land masses of up-thrust magma have appeared—the islets of Palaia and Nea Kameni—which from this angle appear as one low, deserted island of black rock. This whole desolate and beautiful scene is the remnant of what was probably the largest volcanic explosion in human history. The island was once a mountainous, roughly circular land mass, similar in shape and size to Ios, up until the middle of the 2nd millennium BC. Then, in a series of successive cataclysms, the volcanic core of the centre of the island erupted, ejecting up to sixty cubic kilometres of incandescent pumice and ash into the atmosphere. The cone and its magma chamber subsequently collapsed, allowing the sea to pour in through massive breaches to the west, filling the central core.

The depth of the water immediately below the cliffs is so great that it does not permit boats to anchor: they have to tie-up to floating buoys instead, which are chained to the floor of the sea at a depth of nearly 200m. The floor of the caldera lies generally between 200m and 400m below sea level, reaching its deepest points to the north and east of Asprónisi, and directly west and below the crest at Imerovígli where the dry land rises in a cliff to 320m:

this represents a total drop between clifftop and seabed of over 700m.

The black and barren islands of the Ka[i]meni (meaning *burnt*) in the centre of the caldera are the result of the slow and continuing up-thrust of solidified magma. They first appeared in the 2nd century BC, and have grown in circumference, subsided, partially disappeared, re-appeared, split and joined in a constant ballet of movement over the centuries. They represent the focus and dome of the active volcano today, and are currently growing in height and size by a slow process of extrusion from below.

The volcanic eruption

The clearly-defined and variedly-coloured strata of the cliff-face as seen from the water are a legible section through the geological history of the island, showing that the island had been volcanically active for centuries before the 'Great' eruption. The uppermost layers give vulcanologists a picture of the various stages of that final cataclysm. It appears to have taken place over several months—perhaps even more than a year, beginning with premonitory tremors which gave the prehistoric inhabitants of the island warning to leave. There appear to have been moments of quiescence, in which the inhabitants returned to repair damage to their buildings, before being forced to leave once again on a journey which almost certainly culminated later in a gruesome death, even if they had managed to reach dry land on Crete. The final stages were a crescendo of eruptions covering the island with increasingly large volcanic debris settling to ever greater depths on the surface. As the core of the island was destroyed, a column of volcanic ash and steam was ejected into the atmosphere to a height of over thirty kilometres, where the lightest particles were distributed through the stratosphere by currents of air. The heavier tephra, also carried on a prevailing northwest wind, was spread over the southeast Aegean: deposits of up to a metre in depth have been found, for example, on the island of Rhodes.

The immediate effects of this cataclysm can be understood by an invaluable point of comparison: the well-documented eruption of Krakatoa in Indonesia in 1883. After Krakatoa's explosion, darkness lasting more than a day covered an area in excess of four hundred kilometres from the eruption: closer to the epicentre, the impenetrable darkness (of a kind described also by Pliny in relation to the comparatively tiny eruption of Vesuvius) lasted for three days. The colour of skies especially at sunset was affected all over the world; the changes were observed in London, and the sky's unworldly hue is frequently referred to by Theodore Bent in the accounts of his last visits to the Cyclades in the winter of 1884. As a result of the destruction of Krakatoa, over 36,000 people lost their lives and more than 300 villages were destroyed on neighbouring Java. The most dramatic damage was caused by the tidal surges and tsunami: waves in excess of 30m in height radiated out from the epicentre, carrying, in one case, a gun-boat which was moored in a harbour eighty kilometres north of Krakatoa, a distance of over three kilometres inland. The caldera left by the eruption of Krakatoa is between one quarter and one third of the size of that at Santorini; so the effects reliably recounted of its eruption need considerably magnifying when we are considering the eruption of Santorini. The immediate effect of this on Crete, ninety five kilometres to its south, is not hard to imagine: its coastal villages must have been destroyed along with all its harboured sea-craft; its coastal fields would have been inundated and then rendered impracticable for a long period by the layer of ash, and its buildings shaken down by the alternating tremors and blasts from across the water.

Dating the eruption

These historically significant effects on Crete and Minoan civilisation make it vitally important to understand precisely when the eruption of Santorini occurred. It was a hypothesis that the cataclysm was directly responsible for the sudden demise of the Minoan world in the Late Bronze Age that spurred Spyros Marinatos to excavate at Akrotiri in the first place, and to make the discoveries he did (*see below*). He surmised, and produced good evidence from pottery-styles in support of his theory, that the eruption occurred around 1500 BC, that it crippled and destroyed the Palace Culture of Crete and created a vacuum which the ever-opportunistic Mycenaeans then filled. One scholar, Hans Goedicke, wanted to bring the date further forward to 1477 BC: his desire was to make it coincide with the date required by a pharaonic inscription of the reign of Tutmosis III which seems to describe the events of the crossing of the Red Sea by the Israelites (known to us best from *Exodus 14, vv. 15–31*) from the Egyptian point of view. In this way, he suggested, we can explain the extraordinary phenomenon of the sea withdrawing and then returning to crush the Egyptian forces as a consequence of tidal displacements and tsunami caused by the eruption of Santorini.

Recent research has called for a radical adjustment to these estimates, however. The dust propelled into the stratosphere in an eruption of such magnitude causes a period of global cooling, with a parallel reduction in the growth of trees. Dendro-chronologists have noted both narrow growth rings among oaks preserved in the bogs of Ireland and in fossilised bristle-cone pines in California for the period corresponding to the decade following 1628 BC. This date is corroborated by examination of signs of increased acidity in the Greenland ice sheet, which Danish geologists date to c. 1645 BC, ± 20 years. Furthermore, recent radio-carbon dating of seeds and wood found in the ash on Santorini itself, allows for a date of no later than 1600 BC. The fact that the storage jars for grain at Akrotiri (*see p. 28*) are usually found almost empty when excavated, suggests that the eruption may have taken place shortly before the time of the island's early harvest in June. Until new evidence persuasively suggests otherwise, we are safest to assume that the eruption occurred around **1625 BC**, and that, although its effect on Crete and the other neighbouring islands must have been momentarily devastating, it cannot sensibly be considered more than the first event in a domino chain of consequences over the next two centuries which may have led to the demise of Minoan civilisation. And it has little or nothing to do with the wider collapse of Bronze Age civilisation in the Eastern Mediterranean in the 12th century BC.

Subsequent activity

Some sources suggest that an eruption in the 3rd century BC separated Therasía from the northwest of Thera. Strabo vividly describes (*Geography, I, 57*) another eruption in probably 197–96 BC, in which the island, then called *Hiera* and now known as Palaia Kameni, first appeared from under the sea as '*flames burst out from the sea for a period of four days, causing the water to seethe and flare up*' as the island slowly emerged. In 46 AD, another islet, *Thia*, appeared and vanished (Pliny). 726 AD, saw another violent eruption, creating the northeastern lobe of Palaia Kameni. In 1570 the south coast of Santorini, with the port of *Eleusis*, collapsed beneath the sea. Mikra Kameni appeared in 1573, and Nea Kameni in 1707–11. In 1866 a protracted eruption lasted for two years, observed by the French geologist and archaeologist, Ferdinand Fouqué, whose book *Santorini et ses Eruptions* (*see p. 106*), is a mine of information on the island's past volcanic activity: an island, named *Aphroessa*, appeared in 1868 and then disappeared again. The eruptions of 1925/6 joined Mikra and Nea Kameni into a single land mass. There were further eruptions in 1939/40 and 1950; and in July 1956, an earthquake destroyed more than half the buildings in the towns of Oia and Firá.

ATLANTIS: THE ERUPTION IN MYTH

The collective memory of a catastrophe of such dimensions can live on for centuries in the minds and literature of mankind. The floods and momentarily altered sea-levels caused by the sinking of Santorini could possibly lie behind the ancient Greek myth of Deucalion in which Zeus, in his wrath at the vice of man, floods the world saving only two people, Deucalion and his wife Pyrrha. Perhaps the most vivid recollection has lived on in the story of the sunken civilisation of Atlantis. All our 'information' about Atlantis comes from two dialogues of Plato, the *Timaeus* and the unfinished *Critias*, written at the turn of the 4th century BC. In them Plato refers to a conversation between Solon and a venerable Egyptian priest who tells the Greek sage the story of the ideal, proto-civilisation of Atlantis, with its virtuous people and methods of government. It ruled an area, he says, encompassing much of the southeastern Mediterranean, even though the continent itself was placed by Plato, somewhat counter-intuitively, beyond the pillars of Hercules (Straits of Gibraltar). When the people of Atlantis later became arrogant and no longer respected their gods they were beset with wars until finally 'in a single day and night', after violent earthquakes and floods, the island-continent disappeared into the depths of the sea. Similar 'morals' occurs in far earlier Babylonian literature (the *Epic of Gilgamesh*) and in Hebrew literature (*Genesis*); and Flood-myths are common also to Indian, Persian, Chinese, Islamic and Pre-Columbian traditions. But the particular fate of Atlantis as described by Plato, as well as his emphasis on its prosperity and sphere of influence, do suggest that the memory of a glorious Bronze Age civilisation in Greek waters and the catastrophe of Thera are important elements in the weave.

FIRA, THE KAMENI ISLETS AND THE NORTH OF THE ISLAND

(Metropolis Church in Chora = 0.00km for distances in text)

Firá: southern sector and the Museum of Prehistoric Thera

Firá/Chora stretches to either side of a main, cobbled alley which follows the summit of the central eastern ridge of the caldera from south to north. To the east are the newer buildings, on the gentler slope; to the west are the older parts of the town, cut into the volcanic deposit on ledges overlooking the caldera below from a height of 230m. The southern end of the settlement is dominated by the **church of the Panaghia Ypapantis** (the Purification of the Virgin) which is the *Metropolis* or Orthodox cathedral of Santorini, rebuilt after its predecessor was destroyed in the earthquake of 1956. The earthquake wrought widespread damage to most of the buildings in Chora and Oia: the attractive churches down the slope to the west—the (originally 15th-century) **Aghios Minas** to the south, the 17th-century **Aghios Ioannis Theologos**, settled securely into the cliff directly below, and the 19th-

century **church of Aghia Irini** further to the north—all
had to be rebuilt at that time. Their succession of steep
cupolas against the sweep of the caldera has become
one of the most famous images of the island. There are
also several examples of older, traditional **houses** on the
panoramic west slope. They are cut back into the soft deposit of tephra which caps the island at this point, their
rooms excavated into the cliffside and roofed always with
a vaulted ceiling: the volcanic 'rock' hardens when cut and
exposed, and the form of the vault ensures against collapse. This was a more practical method of creating liv-
ing-spaces than sinking foundations into the soft tephra
for erecting buildings above ground. Firá is also particularly exposed to winds in the winter, and the troglodyte
dwellings are windproof and warm, even if they do not
allow easily for fireplaces. External ovens in the small yard
in front of the entrance were a frequent feature, and heat-
ing in the interior generally had to be effected by braziers.

To the north and south ends of Chora, and equidistant
from the centre, are the island's two museums of archaeology. In the south is the **Museum of Prehistoric Thera***
(*open 8–7.30 except Mon*), which opened in 2000 and occupies the new building just below the southeast corner
of the church of the Metropolis. It is an exceptional and
beautifully displayed collection, essential to the proper

understanding of the prehistoric site at Akrotiri (*see p. 70*). The exhibits are arranged in chronological order around three sides of a closed, central court. If you go early in the morning as it opens, you will probably have the museum to yourself for a good half an hour.

A number of the most striking pieces displayed— pieces of furniture, in particular—are plaster 'positives' taken from the negative impression in the lava left by the disintegrated object. The Bronze Age city at Akrotiri was destroyed by the volcanic eruption of the island, and the objects of organic material in its buildings were slowly incinerated by the heat of packed volcanic ash. The ash then hardened with subsequent rainfall, bearing the exact negative impression of the incinerated objects in its form, while the objects themselves slowly disintegrated into dust. The archaeologists were therefore able to reconstruct accurately the forms of many domestic objects, by injecting a plaster-cement into the negative space left by the disintegrated object and then clearing the ash from around it.

Right-hand wing: In the first alcove to the right of the entrance, following the rare examples of fossilised olive leaves* (*Case 1, nos. 1–6*) from c. 60,000 BC, which are the earliest such examples from the Mediterranean area, are objects (*Case 2*) of **Neolithic Cycladic marble-work**—cups, lamps (collared jars), querns, and figurines—showing that settlement was already well-established on the island by the 3rd millennium BC. The obsidian tools used to work the marble are also exhibited. In *Case 3*, we see the characteristic forms and pure designs of Theran pottery emerging in the Early Cycladic period: jars with the pulled-back neck, decorated with simple, confident, abstract designs. In the Middle Cycladic pottery, we begin to see the first **'nipple jars' with exquisite decoration of swallows*** (*nos. 101, 102 & 138*)—a kind of domestic

pottery decorated with symbols of the returning cycle of seasons and the fertility they bring. Opposite, against the wall, is a very fine, shallow **marble basin*** dating from c. 2200 BC.

The **model** of the site of Akrotiri provides a bird's-eye view of the small area of the city so far excavated: the plan of the streets and the small squares, such as the triangular public space in front of the West House, can be appreciated in their similarity to Cycladic villages of today.

Beyond (*Case 4*) are displayed finds from Bronze Age Thera, including the remarkable reconstitutions of **pieces of furniture*** (*nos. 144–45*) taken from the negative impression left by the piece in the hot volcanic ash at the time of the eruption. The ornate design of the table legs (uncannily reminiscent of French 18th-century furniture) is striking. Also exhibited are intriguing **domestic items**—standing lamps, a portable cooking oven, clay firedogs and andirons in the form of oxen, for the cooking of meat over embers, all dating from the 17th century BC. *Case 5* exhibits large **bronze dishes** and weapons, including a **dagger** with gold decoration applied to the surface. There is another reconstitution from the negative impression left by a burnt **woven fruit basket**. Beside, is a fine clay **bathtub**—precursor to a long tradition of such objects in early Greece.

Rear Wing, First Bay: In the centre of the back wall are three magnificent **storage *pithoi***, with different designs on their front faces which perhaps denote the contents: the impressionistic barley-shoot for stored grain, the splash for stored oil, and the circle and cross for wine (the latter appropriately has a spout at its foot). To either side (*Cases 6 & 7*) are **lead weights and measures** for commerce; fragments of inventory tablets in Linear A; and Late Cycladic, spouted jars. In *Case 8* (opposite the *pithoi*) a large collection of **seal-stones** gives an intimation of the organisation and extent of trade contacts which the city had.

Rear Wing, Second Bay: In the central case is a beautiful **ceramic tripod-altar with designs of dolphins*** (*no. 253*). The fact that this was found by Spyros Marinatos in one of the upper rooms of the West House at Akrotiri, at exactly the point where the trajectories of two pictorial narratives of the walking boys carrying fishes for offering meet, confirms its ritual nature as a portable offering-table. The exhibits around are dedicated to **painting fragments** and **examples of pigments**—ferric oxides, earth colours and an imported, Egyptian frit (copper silicate and calcium). The mastery and confidence of line and form, enhanced by bold colours, are striking. The corner is occupied by a reconstruction of a room from the House of the Ladies: the paintings are of **papyrus plants and female figures*** dressed in fine-coloured clothes with make-up and jewellery. The sense of an easeful and prosperous society is conveyed through an artistic maturity and admirable simplicity of design: there is no hesitancy, but utter confidence in the sweeping lines and bright colours.

Opposite, are more storage *pithoi* **with dolphins**

and lilies* (*nos. 271–72*)
in designs of particular
beauty (perhaps sug-
gesting ritual rather than
commercial use). *No. 360*,
which is of more elegant
shape, bears depictions of
gulls and dolphins on one
side, and goats and bulls
on the other, images which
may have related to the
wall-paintings in the room
where it was found.

Left-hand wing: This area
(*Case 9*) exhibits a magnificent array of **Theran
pottery of the 17th cen-
tury** BC, with its unflagging
repertoire of decorations
with both abstract and
floral motifs, swallows
and marine animals: good
examples of both form and
brilliant decoration are

nos. 345 and 346. Note also
the ingenious flower-pots
(*nos. 350–51*) designed so
as to prevent the soil from
dehydrating, and a kind of
strainer, *no. 357*, elegantly
decorated with swallows
in flight. Note also the fine
ritual vessels beautifully
modelled in the forms of
conch shells or the heads of
boar. *Case 10* gives a clear
picture of the geographical
extent of Thera's trading
links, through the im-
ported objects found in the
excavations, which come
from mainland Greece,
Crete, Egypt and the Mid-
dle East: note especially
the Syro-Palestinian pieces,
the **Canaanite jar**, and
the beautiful **Egyptian,
ostrich-egg *rhyton***. Such
trade could only have been

possible in a prevailingly peaceful environment in the Eastern Mediterranean in the 18th and 17th centuries BC.

In the final corner (to left of the entrance) the painted **frieze of the *Blue Monkeys*** from House B has been reconstructed and 'completed' from dozens of fragmentary pieces. Once again the chromatic range, and a confident, simplicity of form, worthy of Matisse, are striking: there is a constantly varying gamut of poses of this lithe and expressive animal, which here, as in Egypt, may have been considered a sacred animal and ministrant of the divinity. Even if monkeys were not native to Thera, the Theran merchants will have seen them in Africa (the surprise at finding them in Cretan painting had led Arthur Evans erroneously to restore a monkey as a child in one segment of painting at Knossos). The last showcase exhibits the only object of precious metal to have been found so far at Akrotiri: a **gold ibex** (hollow-cast in the lost-wax method) found in 1999 inside a wooden box, within a clay chest close to a pile of goat's horns. The piece may have been an import from the Near East.

THERAN PAINTINGS

The clear, simple compositions of Theran painting mark an important step forward in the development of Western Art. They represent a moment in which the history of painting in Europe, deriving from a common origin in Egypt, first begins to acquire characteristics which distinguish it as something we can call 'western'. In earliest times in Egypt, painting was writing and vice versa; and the Egyptian tradition remains steadfastly one in which information and image are inseparable. The idea of a painting as a 'picture'—something which lies so deep in the Western concept of art that we tend to take it for granted—begins first to appear in these Bronze Age murals from Thera and their contemporaries on Crete. The Theran paintings are first and foremost sacred narratives, but they are also remarkable compositions of nature. Indicative of this compositional sense are the large areas of empty space which separate the figures in the scenes of *Young Women Gathering Saffron*, in the museum in Firá: there is no clutter, no unnecessary decoration, just absolute clarity of line and simplicity of colour. The overall proportion of figures to the total area is something quite new: they do not dominate the space, and are amply separated from one another. Only a few examples of Theran painting are on show in Santorini; but the famous murals of the *Two Antelopes*, or of the *Landscape of Lilies with Swallows*, both currently in Athens, are at least visible, in life-size reproduction, at the Petros Nomikos Centre in Firá (*see below*). These, too, are skillful compositions and simplified 'pictures', by comparison with their complex Egyptian forebears which are full of hieroglyphic writing. This does not mean that they did not possess important sacred content for the Therans: they did. But they are conceived compositionally according to new and forward-looking principles. Western art has tended to move forward by repeated processes of simplification, and Theran art represents one such movement.

It should be recalled that the murals from Akrotiri are not the only examples we have of wall-paintings of their epoch: there are others which come from Crete and later examples from mainland Greece. But they are among the most complete and beautiful to have been found so far, and they possess, by virtue of the conditions in which they were found, a clearer architectural context than the others, which helps us to understand their meaning. They were created, as the museum displays show, in simple iron-oxide earth pigments, available in abundance on the island. Only the blue—a synthetic pigment or 'frit', made from copper silicate and calcium—was imported from Egypt. The painting technique cannot be called pure 'fresco', because, although the painter may have begun painting into the wet, calcium hydroxide plaster, much of the descriptive detail is executed in tempera on the dry surface.

Firá/Chora: northern sector & Old Archaeological Museum

A short climb from the centre, following the main pedestrian street, brings you to the (Old) **Archaeological Museum** (*open daily 8.30–3, except Mon*), close to the cable car terminal. Although there are some prehistoric finds on show, the collection principally exhibits objects of the historic periods from around the island.

The entrance area displays those prehistoric finds from Akrotiri which were made between 1899 and 1908, with their characteristic clear and open, decorative designs: a fine Middle Cycladic *pithos* **with lily-design** stands opposite the entrance, beside two others with abstract designs. By comparison with them, the designs on the objects from the Late Geometric period, and 8th and 7th centuries BC, in the first **main gallery** (*to the left*), are tight and methodical, lacking the spontaneity and fluidity of their Bronze Age predecessors: it is instructive to see the two epochs juxtaposed here. The many examples of slip-painted, large **burial amphora** exhibited along the walls of the gallery, which were produced locally on the island, are decorated with particularly fine geometric designs nonetheless. One exceptional *pithos* (*at the left end*), dating from c. 675 BC and of typical Cycladic design, has an embossed, **relief decoration**, depicting (on the neck of the vase) a swan preening its tail-feathers, and below, winged horses drawing chariots. The centrepiece of the collection of artefacts which come from the cemeteries of Ancient *Thera* (*see p. 43*), is the **clay figurine of a mourning woman*** of Daedalic style (*no. 392, in a case on its own, immediately on the left on entering*), dating from the late 7th century BC. It has survived intact, with the colours and features excellently preserved: it is decorated only on the front face. The gesture of the hands raised to the head expresses lamentation. The several fragmentary and eroded **kouroi** in the room, which have often vigorous modelling of the hair, show how in the 7th century BC artistic creativity was at its most powerful in the plastic arts of carving and modelling. These *kouroi* would have stood, larger than life, as grave-markers.

In the **second gallery** (*to the right*), the central case displays some very fine, late 6th-century BC, ceramic-ware imported from Attica: a **black-figure *kylix****, exquisitely decorated with ships around the rim, and mythical and battle scenes, designed with a perfect overall balance of intricate figures and empty space. The piece is inscribed with the name of its owner on the outer rim. Next to it a vase unusually depicts horses, both in profile, and viewed front-on. The last case displays votive and funerary offerings, including many **zoömorphic vases** and perfume-jars in the forms of dolphins, ducks and doves. The collection concludes with a number of marble Hellenistic busts and heads from the public spaces of Ancient *Thera*.

The museum looks onto a small square to its north. To the left, the path passes the terminus of the **cable car** which descends to the old port; the journey takes three minutes. It was built in 1979 by the (Austrian) Doppelmayr company, and was the gift of the Greek shipping magnate and benefactor, Evangelos Nomikos. By continuing past the terminus and climbing up the path which follows the edge of the rim, you come to a large red, **neoclassical mansion** on a projecting corner, which houses the **Petros Nomikos Centre**, the creation of another member of the same family. The handsome building dating from the end of the 19th century, was damaged in 1956 and then restored thirty years later according to its original appearance. The complex of tunnels in the rock behind which were cellars for wine-storage, now houses the permanent exhibition of '**Theran Wall-paintings in Photographic Reproduction**' (*open daily 10–9*), covering all the paintings so far discovered at Akrotiri, most of whose originals are in Athens. The path continues beyond the building to **Firostefáni** (literally, the 'crown of Firá'), the attractive and panoramic northern extremity of Chora.

Continuing instead straight ahead (*north*) from the square in front of the (Old) Archaeology Museum, you come to the Venetian, Catholic quarter of Chora. The 18th-century **Ghisi Mansion** (or *Megaro Gyzi*), one block to the north, has a fine, vaulted courtyard. It houses a **Historical Museum** (*open daily May–Oct 10.30–1 & 5–8; Sun 10.30–4.30*) exhibiting prints and engravings of Santorini from the 17th to the 19th century, and an interesting collection of photographs of the island's buildings before and after the 1956 earthquake. There is a small collection of paintings and archive material from the Catholic

Bishopric. Immediately to the west is the Roman Catholic **Cathedral of the Immaculate Conception** (1823), now restored to pristine condition after the damage wrought by the earthquake of 1956: its ornate **bell-tower** is a fine piece of Italianate, Cycladic architecture. Close by are the Dominican Convent of the Rosary and the Catholic Bishop's residence.

The old port, and the volcano on the Kameni Islets

A zig-zag of six hundred steps descends from the bottom edge of Kato Firá (*west from the main crossing of alleys at the centre of Chora*) down to the **Old Port**, 230m below, which is sometimes referred to as Skala Firás, or simply as Ormos. Donkeys and mules carry people up and down, preserving a long-standing tradition. When the cable car opened, it was agreed that a portion of every ticket sold would be given as a subsidy to the muleteers, so that the tradition could be maintained. The harbour below is tiny and the water black in colour.

From the quay, excursion trips leave for the 'volcano' and the **Kameni Islands** opposite, in the centre of the Caldera: these can be arranged through the Dakoutros Travel Agency in Firá (*T: 22860 22958*). The islands are magma domes, which have pushed up in successive eruptions to a height of 130m above the water level. Both Strabo and

Seneca describe the first appearance of Palaia Kameni from the water in 197–96 BC, using the common source of Posidonius who may have derived his information from an eyewitness of the event. Something of the tortuous history and shifting size and height of this mass of solidified magma is traced above (*see under Volcanic Caldera on pp. 14ff*). From the (usual) point of disembarkation on the north side of **Nea Kameni**, which corresponds to the area of the island which first appeared in 1570, a path leads up to the summit above the central crater of the volcano, which exhibits little visible activity beyond the escape of a strong and stinging sulphurous vapour. Nothing lives or grows on the island. Close to the shore, the land mass is formed of boulders of shiny, black basalt with forms that are alternately slickly rounded and jagged-edged. From the summit, the cooled magma flows of the last major eruptions can be distinguished: the 1707–11 deposits to the northwest; the main 1925–28 deposits to the east; and the massive areas of the 1866–70 deposits to the south. On the surface to the west the superimposed lava flows of 1925–28 can be seen. **Warm springs** rise under water at several points near both Palaia and Nea Kameni. Most excursions stop near the chapel of the Taxiarch on Nea Kameni: the shoreline is coloured red from the minerals in the springs, which rise from the seabed at c. 35°C. It is necessary to swim some distance in cold water from where the boat stops, before reaching the area of the springs. The heat dissipates quickly in the surrounding water.

Imerovígli to Oia

Although a separate community, **Imerovígli** (2.5km) is today almost a continuation of Chora and Firostefáni. At 320m above sea level, it occupies the highest point of the perimeter rim of the caldera, with comparably commanding views. Its two principal religious buildings, the 17th-century **convent of Aghios Nikolaos** to the south, and the **church of the Panaghia Maltesa** on the main square, were both restored or rebuilt after the earthquake of 1956, though the latter still preserves the finely-carved **wooden iconostasis** of the church that it replaced. A stepped footpath leads west out of Imerovígli, across a col, to the red, eroded **rock-stack of Skaros**; this was the dramatic, and now abandoned, site chosen by the Venetian overlord, Giacomo Barozzi to build his fortress and 'capital' when he was given possession of the island by Marco Sanudo in 1207. Eighteenth-century engravings (Choiseul-Gouffier and Fauvel) show it as a populous settlement with reputedly 200 habitations, mostly for the Catholic and Venetian community. A bell on the summit warned of any imminent danger from pirates. In the 18th century, the erosion and impracticality of the site prompted the families to leave and settle further south at Chora and at Pyrgos. An English visitor in 1850 described the houses '*perched one over another where a crevice in the sides of the precipice will admit, and in the most frightful positions*'. He claimed there was then only one living inhabitant. Today the ruined walls of a few buildings, churches and the stepped street are all that remain.

The road from Imerovígli to Oia (best taken in the early morning before the island is awake) follows the ridge of the rim, with superb **views*** over the slopes to the east, and at intervals down into the caldera. Other islands are visible on all sides: Folegandros and Sikinos in the west, Naxos and Ios to the north, and Amorgos and Anaphi in the east. The strata in the walls of the cliff beside the road are a visible history of the evolution of the great eruption. At the eastern extremity of Oia is the separate community of **Phoinikiá** to the north of the road: its small, rock-cut **church of Aghios Giorgios**, dates probably from the 13th century and contains murals from the same period, currently under conservation.

Oia* (11km; pronounced 'Ee-a'), which commands the northern entry into the caldera, was the island's principal commercial centre up until the Second World War.

It is a quieter and more picturesque settlement than Firá, affording a different perspective on the caldera. As viewed from the church of Aghios Nikolaos, looking east, it is a unique tissue of habitation: its varied forms and colours of houses—some still derelict from the 1956 earthquake—flow along the summit of the ridge in a succession of half-cylinders, rectangles and occasional hemispheres, interspersed with the irregular flights of steps that link them. The appearance is more plastic and sculptural than linear. The houses are constructed in rough volcanic rocks, cemented with the island's abundant *pozzolana*, and then thickly plastered to give a neat and uniform surface. At the highest level, there are several **neoclassical captains' houses**, characterised by a substantial blind attic on the façade which serves to mask the high, vaulted ceilings behind which were designed to keep the interiors as cool as possible. In one of the finest of these mansions, towards the western end of the town, is the **Nautical Museum** (*open 10–3 except Tues*), containing a number of fine carved ship's **figureheads**, maritime memorabilia, models, watercolours, and ship's equipment. On the point at the western extremity of the town is the 15th-century Venetian *Kastro*, with strategic surveillance to north and east, and over the entirety of the caldera to the south. Below Oia, accessible either by road or by two flights of steps, is the **Harbour of Amoudi**, overhung by russet-red cliffs of lava. Boats depart from the quay here twice daily to cross to Therasía (*see below*).

An alternative, little-used route returns to Chora, via Tholós, Aghia Irini and Vourvoúlos. The landscape is wide and open, and terraced for cultivating the legumes and pulses for which the island is famous, and which are able to resist the winds that hit this part of the island with particular force. The older churches in the land-scape around **Tholos** (11.5km) are also sunk low into the ground for protection. The island's northeastern slopes are creased with seasonal torrent beds that cut deeply into the soft soil in ravines. In one such 'crease' between the tiny harbour of Aghia Irini and Vourvoúlos is the mon-astery **church of Aghios Artemios**: its broad *catholicon*, and the surrounding older buildings, cut and constructed into the hillside around an irregular space, give a momen-tary glimpse of how Santorini looked before the concrete boom.

THE SOUTH OF THE ISLAND

Mesaria, Episkopí Goniás and Kamarí

The road east from Chora towards the airport descends to **Mesariá** (3km), which grew up as an important agricultural centre for wine production on the island. At Vóthonas, to the south of the settlement, is a **Wine Museum**, created in the underground caves of a winery, displaying some of the technology and history of wine-making on the island since the 17th century. Landmarks of Mesariá are its grand, early **neoclassical mansions** built by the island's entrepreneurs and merchants in the late 19th century—the decaying **Saliveros Mansion**, and the recently restored **Argyros Mansion**, built by a successful wine-merchant in 1888, whose interior is open for public visits, from May to October (*information: T. 22860 31669*). East of Mesariá the road continues to the airport (4.5km) and to **Monólithos** (6km) which takes its name from the conspicuous landmark of a high outcrop of rock, visible to the east of the airport. The rock appears to have been the focus for a Mycenaean presence on the island in the 12th century BC.

The right-hand branch at the principal junction between Mesariá and the airport leads towards Kamári and

Ancient *Thera*, passing east of Vóthonas and **Exo Goniá** which are interesting settlements for their stacked, traditional, troglodyte architecture. In the area there was an Archaic *Heroön* to Achilles in antiquity. At **Episkopí Goniás** (5km) another right branch leads one kilometre up to the **church of the Panaghia Episkopí** on the lower slopes of Mount Prophitis Elias. This is the most interesting and important church on the island and contains paintings and architectural features comparable with the finest on Naxos. The church, which was the seat of the Orthodox bishop of the island in the Byzantine period, is built on the base of an Early Christian Basilica of the 6th century, and may have been the *catholicon* of a monastery which no longer exists. It was badly damaged by fire in 1915, but a number of the most important paintings have fortunately survived.

The existing structure was founded in 1115 by Alexius I Comnenus of Byzantium, who had also sanctioned the building of the Monastery of St John on Patmos. The small, domed, inscribed-cross design is built over the sanctuary of the Early Christian basilica; the **apse** and ***synthronon*** of the earlier building are maintained in the 12th-century structure. The church is entered through a barrel-vaulted narthex; two openings lead into the *naos* which is compact and high. In its centre are two **columns**

supporting the dome which are probably unchanged in position from the early basilica, and are composed of several elements: the column to the north stands on an ancient altar as its base, and has an unusual, Early Christian, Doric-style capital; that to the south has, in addition, a second altar with carved garlands and *bucrania* incorporated just below the capital. The side aisles have a mixture of fluted and plain antique columns.

The majority of the **wall paintings*** are in the south side; they date from the early 12th century and are in a highly individual style, characterised by clear, sharp forms, minimal design, and pale colours. The eyes of the figures are unusually widely-spaced. On the south wall of the south bay is the *Dormition of the Virgin*, in which Apostles, animated by dismay, look on; to the left (*east wall*), is a *Virgin* of the Blachernae type, with a strikingly young and princely Christ; to the right is the *Resurrection*. In the arch over the passage into the south bay the subject is *Salomé with the head of the Baptist, and Herod enthroned*, in which the faces and costumes are executed with remarkable delicacy. There are less well-preserved murals in the north side, and figures of Apostles in the conch of the sanctuary. In the southwest corner of the *naos* is the famous, **12th-century processional icon** of the *Virgin Glykophilousa*. The shadowed eyes and highly stylised faces are set off by a rich, red background: the angels and figures in the border are also of particularly fine execution.

The most unusual element of the interior is the rare, **keromastic decoration of the marble *templon* screen**. The spaces between the outlines of the abstract and foliate decorative patterns have been carved out, and the cavities filled with a paste made from (iron oxide) earth-pigments and wax. The surface has then been polished, giving an effect of great richness and beauty.

Many **ancient *spolia*** are included in the exterior of the church: outside the northeast corner is a section of trabeation with metopes and triglyphs, and pieces of cornice, as well as one massive, ancient threshold block in red volcanic rock made into a table, supported by two Early Christian *templon* elements.

East of the turning for the church of the Episkopí, the road continues to **Kamári** (7km) an expanding resort set behind a long beach of black volcanic sand. On several plots in the town, where archaeologists have been able to make salvage excavations before building has begun, traces of the port of Ancient *Oea* have come to light. Theodore Bent visited Kamári in 1883 and remarks on seeing '*the remains of a Roman temple, some statues of inferior workmanship, and the foundations of houses*'. *Oea* was founded in the 8th century BC as the out-port for the main settlement of Ancient *Thera* which crowns the mountain to the south.

ANCIENT (HISTORIC) THERA

Open daily 8.30–3 except Mon.

The siting of **Ancient *Thera*** is one of the most audacious in the Aegean. It occupies the exposed, eastern spur of Mount Prophitis Elias, known as Mesa Vouno, looking across the water to Anaphi. To the west rises the island's highest summit; on all other sides the mountain drops over 300m, straight to the sea. The Prophitis Elias protrusion is the only solid limestone on the island where foundations can be sunk into rock rather than into volcanic pumice. The remains of the city are interesting and varied: it was the only large settlement on the island in early historic times—not to be confused with the prehistoric city whose remains are at Akrotiri (*see below*). Access by foot is arduous: either by an unrelenting, thirty-minute climb up a switchback road from Kamári (*on the north side*), or by a rough track from Períssa (*on the south side*); there are no buses but taxis will, somewhat reluctantly, take visitors to the top of the road. These two paths converge on a narrow saddle, which was occupied by the

ancient cemeteries of the city, between the summit of Prophitis Elias (567m) and the acropolis of the ancient town (366m) to the east.

HISTORY

The city was founded and settled around the 9th or 8th century century bc, by Dorians from Laconia, under a Spartan leader, Theras. The site was strategically placed to dominate the maritime routes both between Crete and the Aegean, and between the Greek and Asia Minor mainlands. Below the mountain were harbours both to the north and south side, one or other of which afforded protection whatever the direction of the wind. The principal harbour was the settlement of Ancient *Oea* (modern Kamári) to the north, founded probably at the same time as the city on the mountain above. The settlement of *Eleusis* to the south, at the harbour of modern Vlycháda, seems to be a Hellenistic foundation, however: the geographer and astronomer, (Claudius) Ptolemy, writing in the 2nd century AD, mentions both ports by name, but curiously does not refer to *Thera*. The finds from the Geometric and Archaic cemeteries of the city show that *Thera* knew considerable prosperity early on. Herodotus recounts that, after a protracted drought of several years around 630 bc, the city was forced to found a colony of its own, at Cyrene on the North African coast. This was its only colony, but one which grew to unforeseen wealth and importance. *Thera*, as was typical of Dorian settlements, was conservative both in its art and its external relations. It only became a truly cosmopolitan centre in Hellenistic times under the rule of the Ptolemies. It is from this period of prosperity that most of the ruins and the plan of the city date.

The site was first examined and the cemeteries excavated by the German scholar, Hiller von Gärtringen, between 1895 and 1903. The next systematic excavation was begun by Greek archaeologists under Nikolaos Zapheiropoulos in the 1960s, and continues today.

Cemeteries

The extensive cemeteries are disposed along the saddle or col which joins Mesa Vouno to the main mountain of Prophitis Elias. Long before reaching the ridge as you climb up on the Kamári side, clear cuts and stepped platforms in the rock reveal the sites of tombs on the hillside to the north of the road, dating largely from Hellenistic times: then in the last few switchbacks, the **bases and**

steps of a wide variety of slightly earlier funerary buildings can be seen, often in different colours of stone—red, white and grey—to either side of the **ancient road** up to the city which is also visible in stretches. The simplest graves would have been marked with a cube of stone engraved with the name of the deceased; the important early Archaic graves were marked by standing, marble *kouroi*; later ones by small architectural structures. One would have arrived at the city through a forest of funerary monuments, unable to see the habitation yet, but with wide, open views to the sea. On the Veríssa side, just below the enclosure fence of the site, are more **monument bases** again in different colours of stone. The rich finds—statuary, votive gifts and funerary urns—found in these cemeteries are on display in the Archaeological Museum in Chora (*see p. 35*). As recently as November 2000, a fine Daedalic *kore* of the late 7th century BC was uncovered on the south-facing slope: the well-preserved, monolithic statue of a female figure, with long, braided hair, stands 2.3m high, and once marked a tomb. It is a particularly fine piece of early Archaic sculpture.

The Hellenistic city

As you climb towards the remains of the city itself from the entrance to the enclosed area you pass the double-nave **church of Aghios Stephanos**, which dates from perhaps as early as the 9th century AD, and is built within the remains of a 5th century AD **Early Christian basilica**, dedicated to the Archangel Michael. The chapel is constructed with antique material, its vaulted, cave-like interior, reminiscent of Aghios Kosmás on Kythera in the ubiquitous use of ancient *spolia*. Monolithic columns without capitals rudimentarily support the vaults, and ancient blocks and tomb-covers from the Christian basilica, engraved with crosses and inscriptions, constitute parts of the walls. The area of rock behind the church shows signs of quarrying: all the stone in Ancient *Thera*, apart from the elements of white marble and red, volcanic stone, comes from the ridge itself.

Fifty metres beyond Aghios Stephanos you come to the *Temenos* **or Shrine of Artemidoros of Perge**, who was admiral of the Ptolemaic fleet in the late 4th century BC. Little remains of the superstructure of what was a grand and complex monument, intended equally to honour a group of divinities and to promote his own glory. The **carved symbols of the principal divinities** are clearly visible in the rock-face behind: the Dolphin of Poseidon,

the Lion of Apollo and the Eagle of Zeus. Artemidorus—
as sailor and admiral—has had his own image carved in
numismatic profile and positioned above the dolphin of
Poseidon. The cutting away of the platform of the shrine
would have provided stone for construction in the town.

After a final rise with steps, the path drops into the **Agorá** of the city. The area is not built around a central square
as was most common, but is drawn out along the ridge of
the mountain, as determined by the steep lie of the land.
The bases of shops are seen to the seaward side, while the
residential area climbs up above, to the right. This is a
good point at which to observe the variety of masonry:
in the shops are many elements in a dark red, volcanic
pumice brought from the north of the island, which provides vivid chromatic relief; visible on the hillside, well
below to the left, is the perfect, drafted, 4th-century BC
masonry of the corner bastion of a deep podium for a
building on the slope, referred to as the *platys teichos*, or
broad wall. On the hill above the Agorá, the walls display
areas of similarly well-cut and laid ashlar masonry, alternating with other areas of rough and irregular masonry:
the latter would probably have been faced with plaster,
the former left exposed. This meant that the appearance
of the ancient town was not that dissimilar to many historic Mediterranean towns today, in which the corners of

large buildings—which always take the brunt of knocks and bangs—are in clean masonry, while the long stretches of wall were rendered with a *stucco*. On the slope, the public buildings to the seaward side broke the wind, and reflected the stepped buildings facing them higher up. The streets of the area are endowed with a network of covered drains.

A little further along the main path and to the right-hand side is the **Royal Stoa**, an elongated building, with a central spine of columns, running below terraces above. This was a roofed and closed edifice, built at the start of the 1st century AD, which functioned as the city's principal civic and judicial building. The central columns supported a hipped roof which (according to inscriptions) collapsed in an earthquake during the reign of Trajan and had to be restored. The building would have exhibited decrees inscribed on *stelai* similar to those in the back wall of the building, which have been haphazardly immured there at a later date. To the south, the main street narrows, passing a **municipal water-house**, a communal cistern which husbanded the city's precious supply of stored water, to supplement that of the private houses which were nearly all endowed with a cistern for collecting rainwater. To the east of it, opens out the small, highly panoramic, 3rd-century BC **theatre**. This began as a Greek-style theatre with a circular *orchestra* and low *skene*; but, as often happened, it was re-modelled in Roman times with a large *skene* which now took up half the space of the original *orchestra*. The street beyond the theatre leads down between finely built ashlar walls of houses to either side, towards the oldest and most sacred area of the town. Before following it, we retrace our steps to the north end of the Royal Stoa, so as to explore the residential area further uphill.

Residential Quarter (*detour*)

Our route is indicated on the cornerstone of the building above the north end of the Royal Stoa by a large, **engraved phallus,** an optimistic symbol of fortune and prosperity, more than a sexual proposition. The design, in which the circles have been cut using a compass, looks like a later engraving on a panel which had previously eroded. It points significantly to the small, Hellenistic **Temple of Dionysos,** opposite, on the right hand side of the stepped street. In the spaces adjacent to the latter temple, there are fragments of architrave decoration, including a run of triglyphs in marble, which have been unearthed in excavations. At the top of the steps, a path which dog-legs to the right leads across a space occupied by a *gymnasium* to an imposingly large residence with a clearly visible en-

trance atrium, before which sits a 'bomb' of black lava, of
the kind ejected by the volcano when active. This building
was designated arbitrarily the **Governor's Residence**, because of its position at the highest point and its grand *pro-
pylon* or porticoed doorway which marked the entrance
from the street to its east. To the left, from the top of the
steps above the Temple of Dionysos, the street descends
through some of the **best-preserved residential buildings** on the site: one conserves its *foricae* in good condition, and a plastered cistern supported by pillars for stor-
ing the water deriving from an *impluvium* above; others
have coloured **threshold blocks** in red and black volcanic
stone; and most preserve vestiges, at the base of their interior walls, of the red-painted plaster which coated their
surface. Beyond, the path drops down to the **Temple of
Pythian Apollo** of which little remains, beyond a finely
cut **lustral basin**. The building was converted in the 6th
century into an early Byzantine church, whose apse can
be seen to the east. At this point, to south and west, an
immense **view** opens out over the south coast at Eríssa
and Vlycháda, with the mass of the mountain rising in
vertical striations sheer out of the flat, coastal shelf below.
Overlooking this sobering sight is a rock shelf, cut with
an amphitheatre of niches and ledges: this was the **sanctuary of the Egyptian Gods**, deities which included Isis,

Anubis and Serapis, who were imported into the cosmopolitan world of Hellenistic Greece through commerce with Egypt.

The Archaic sanctuaries

Returning again to the Agorá and the theatre, we follow the **Sacred Way** to the southeast, down the ridge of the mountain, to the panoramic promontory where the sacred centre of the Archaic city was built. This area, with its unearthly setting, was the **Sanctuary of the Dorian cult of Apollo *Karneios****. It spreads over a series of terraces, part cut into the rock, part constructed on massive retaining walls which are visible even from Períssa below. All around this platform of rock, is the sea; above, is the sky; ahead, the rising sun, and the island of Anaphi or *Anaphe*, 'the apparition'. The area is overlooked from the northwest by the base of a **temple dedicated to Ptolemy III**, from which the lay-out can be observed: the humped ridge stretches ahead, with the rectangular base of the Temple of Apollo to the left side, and the larger rectangular Terrace of the Ephebes to the right. The latter is where the *Gymnopaidíai* (*see below*), ritual dances and displays performed by ephebes in honour of Apollo during the Karneia festival, took place in the heat of August.

The base of the **Temple of Apollo Karneios** is cut into

the rock of the hillside, with an orientation about 25 degrees off an exact east/west axis: the temple proper is preceded by a *pronaos*, a courtyard and further rooms, in all occupying a space of approximately thirty two metres by ten metres. The **threshold and the door-post slots** of the temple entrance can be seen cut in the rock at the southeast corner. The temple is preceded by a court, with a large cistern below at the northeast side, roofed with limestone beams, which collected the (sacred) water which fell on the temple's roof and precinct. To the right side is possibly a priest's residence: to left, the front of the temple. Two doorways, still intact, lead in from the side of the *naos* through the southwest wall into small rooms that probably functioned as **treasuries**.

The **Terrace of the Ephebes**, also referred to as the Square of the *Gymnopaidíai*, is the long rectangular plat-form to the south of the temple across the ridge of rock, built out over massive **retaining walls of the 6th century** BC, repaired in later periods in the upper areas. These are best seen from below, from where a fine stretch of po-lygonal masonry can also be seen higher up and further to the west. In this exposed area the *Gymnopaidíai* were held in honour of Apollo from at least as early as the 7th century BC. The rocks in between the temple and the ter-race, where the male spectators of these performances sat, are covered with a **wealth of scratched inscriptions and graffiti***, ranging in date from the 7th century BC to later Classical and Hellenistic times. Amongst them are some of the earliest examples of the Greek alphabet in the Aegean. The inscriptions, some of which are quite long, are written all over the rocks in their various Archaic scripts: they record names and erotic appreciations of the boys who performed dances and martial displays here during the festival. There are drawings of heads, abstract patterns, and engraved outlines of feet. The presiding divinities of the boys as they reached adulthood were Hermes (for mental faculties and quickness of wits) and Hercules (for bodily strength and development): on a level below the south corner of the terrace is a deep cave, penetrating the mountainside, which was the **sacred grotto of Hermes and Hercules**. Here, too, there are **inscriptions** all around: from the Archaic period on the left door jamb; two later, Classical ones, higher up; and many more, of Hellenistic times, against the rock face to the left as you look in towards the cave. The surface of the external wall is beautifully finished by hand, with a mason's point. The doorway to the left (*west*) of the cave leads into the remains of **Roman baths**. The rock-cut esplanade in front of the cave constituted the heart of the *Gymnasium* **of the Ephebes**, a structure added in Hellenistic times to the sanctuary.

As you return from the *Gymnasium*, climbing back up towards the Agorá, the view opens out over the coast at Kamári: on the hillside below, in the foreground, about 150m to the north of the Temple of Apollo *Karneios*, is the base of a Hellenistic **Heröon** to an unknown figure. The clear lines of isodomic masonry in its base and walls can be seen below the modern chapel of the *Annunciation* which has been built into it.

GYMNOPAIDIAI

In a famous incident recounted by Herodotus (*Histories, VII, 208–9*), Spartan soldiers, on the eve of the Battle of Thermopylae, were observed by a Persian spy, 'stripped for exercise and dressing and combing their hair': both the spy and his master found the behaviour astonishing. It was later explained to Xerxes by Demaratus—himself a Spartan aristocrat—that 'the Spartans pay careful attention to their hair when they are about to risk their lives.' We, too, share Xerxes's bewilderment: we would not have expected soldiers to have been seen setting their hair before departing for the Battle of Britain (something that suggests that attitudes to warfare have changed out of all recognition between the ancient and modern worlds). The observation is yet more significant because, of all the soldiers of history, the Spartans have the reputation of being the most seriously martial of all.

In a way that recalls aspects of Japanese culture, warfare in the Spartan mind was a sacred art in which the cult and perfection of the male body—its symmetry, its endurance and its performance—were part of a divine calling. This 'cult' meant more than doing physical jerks and running assault courses: it meant ritualising martial actions and physical discipline, and exalting organised movement in a group, which led to a vital subordination of the individual will to the larger unit. It also meant more than seeing the body as a machine—an accusation often made in ignorance against Spartan culture—it meant exalting the strength and endurance of a well-trained body as a divine gift, as an emulation of the most beautiful of gods, Apollo. The Greeks never sacrificed an animal that was not perfect and properly prepared: the Spartans at Thermopylae were not blind to the probability of their imminent self-sacrifice, and accordingly they prepared themselves to be fit for such a divine

calling, by attending carefully to their hair on the eve
of the battle.

Thera was a Spartan colony, and at the main feast
in honour of its presiding divinity, Apollo *Karneios*,
in the month of August, it organised sacred specta-
cles which, like those in Sparta itself, lasted several
days. These were known as the *Gymnopaidíai*, which
as their name implies (γυμνός, 'naked' or 'unarmed';
παίζω, 'I play or disport') were performed, probably
naked, by boys who were passing from childhood
into adulthood. They performed what appear to have
been dances and martial sequences combining both
musical grace and martial skill with the impressive
endurance demanded by performing, as Plato points
out (*Laws, I, p. 633 b&c*), under heat of the August
sun. Only males performed and only men watched.
This was part of a cultural phenomenon in Sparta, in
which it was expected, even insisted on, by tradition
that a young man have an older, male lover who was
his instructor and role model, and that every adult
man be the mentor of an adolescent. Such a relationship was considered necessary for the proper forma-
tion of a young person. Pederasty and military train-

ing are inseparably connected in Lacedaemonian culture. Commentators have traditionally sought to underline the chaste and 'Platonic' nature of this kind of relationship, and in Sparta itself this was probably the case if we believe what Plutarch and Xenophon tell us. Perhaps in Thera it was different, because of a strong influence from neighbouring Crete, whose attitudes to the body were very different from those in Laconia. The Theran inscriptions, scratched into the rocks beside the terrace where the *Gymnopaidíai* took place, occasionally point to something explicitly physical. One often cited example says bluntly: Ἀμο[τ]ίωνα ὤιπ[φ]ε Κρίμων [τ]ε(ῖ)δ[ε]. The use of the Laconian dialectal variant, 'ὤιπε', normally used for animals copulating, suggests that the pleasure taken between Amotion and Krimon was not particularly chaste. The reality of the festival was probably a much more complex one, in which, as always in life, there were baser fringes on the edge of what was a sacred ritual of martial arts. Looking at the elemental setting at *Thera* for these youthful displays—the exposed terrace with nothing but sea below, sky above, the massive rock mountain behind, and the blazing

August sun—it is clear that the *Gymnopaidíai* had a symbolism and significance that resonated far beyond the ephemeral passions of Krimon and his like.

Pyrgos and Prophitis Elias

A newly-built road leads directly south from Chora, along the ridge of the pumice quarries towards Megalochóri. As it begins to climb, the silhouette of **Pyrgos** can be seen to the southeast against the slopes of Mount Prophitis Elias; at 3.5km, a road leads east to the village. It is built in the classic manner of the Cycladic fortified settlement in which a ring of houses, whose outer-facing walls join to form the outer defensive enceinte, surrounds a central hilltop fortress: at Pyrgos, several almost concentric rings of streets ascend the hill in the space between, creating an interesting and attractive ensemble. The four surviving castles on the island, at Oia, Skaros, Akrotiri, and Pyrgos, appear to have been created as a planned, interconnected unity, designed to survey and defend both the approaches to the island as well as its cultivable terrain; all are constructed in the same rough volcanic rock bound in *pozzolana* mortar. Pyrgos is the largest of them all and constituted the principal residence of the rulers and the island's capital after the abandonment of Skaros. The **church of**

the Koimisis (the Dormition) on the western slope of the town, may originally predate the Venetian arrival in 1207, suggesting that there was a Byzantine settlement here before: there are Byzantine and ancient *spolia* incorporated in its exterior walls. At the summit, is the 17th-century **church of the Eisodia tis Theotokou** (the Presentation of the Virgin). Just below, one of the island's largest neoclassical mansions has been restored; it has the characteristic, high attic and *mezzaluna* above the door to maximise a cooling ventilation. The restored **church of Aghia Triada** houses a small **Icon Collection** (*open daily 10–4, Orthodox Easter–Oct*), which date from the 16th to 19th centuries and include works by the Skordilis workshop on Milos. There are also other ecclesiastical items on display which were salvaged from churches in the aftermath of the 1956 earthquake.

Below the summit of the mountain (567m), reached by following through Pyrgos and continuing to the south, is the **Monastery of Prophitis Elias** (9km), founded in 1711 and extensively restored after 1956. The monastery was home to an important 'hidden school' in the first half of the 19th century, keeping alive the Greek language and traditional religious and secular culture during the last years of Turkish occupation. The beauty of the panoramic position has been compromised by the quantity of military and telecommunications hardware at the summit of the mountain.

Emboreio, Perissa and Vlychada

As soon as the road south from Chora crosses the ridge above the new port of Athiniós, the south of the island spreads out below; a patchwork of fields which are stippled with a pointillism of green against a pale background. These are the vineyards of Santorini, which are unique in their method of cultivation: each green dot is an individual vine, which is never husbanded in order to create the usual contiguous lines standing above the ground, but is instead wound round and round upon itself, and kept as low as possible to the ground so as to remain undamaged by the strong winds. Santorini had no particular tradition of viticulture in antiquity that we know of, but since the 16th century has produced wine on a large scale.

Five kilometres from Chora the road reaches **Megalochóri** (5km), the centre of the island's wine production. It is a pleasant village, relatively unvisited, with several fine neoclassical mansions. From the village centre a path leads (*southwest, past the Hotel Artemis*) to **Thérmi**, a point far below on the shore of the caldera where there are natural **hot springs**. The path here gains the rim of the caldera, descends past the **church of Aghios Nikolaos**, cut into the cliff, and eventually arrives at a building made of a series of vaulted chambers. Down the steps beyond, at the shore, the springs rise in a small improvised cabin at c. 35°C.

WINE AND WATER ON SANTORINI

It used to be joked that Santorini had more wine than it had water—an irony borne out by the facts. Water has always been a problem on the island, since the only springs are those under the southern and eastern limestone slopes of Mount Prophitis Elias. For years the island was dependent on daily deliveries of water by ship from the mainland. Now a solar-assisted desalination plant at the north of the island supplies up to nine hundred cubic metres per day, covering most of the daily requirement in the summer season. The volcanic soil, however, produces wine in seemingly unlimited quantities. Volcanic earth provides an ideal habitat for the vine, which appreciates the rapid and efficient drainage it provides, it naturally contains a range of nutritive minerals and, most importantly, it has the capacity to absorb, at a microscopic level, the morning condensation in the air caused by the often considerable change of temperature during the night. It releases these frequent but small supplies of water to the roots, in what are ideal conditions for vine growth. The curious method of weaving the vine into a cylindrical 'basket' close to the level of the ground— almost unique to Santorini—minimises both evaporation in the heat of the day and damage from the frequent winds that sweep over the surface of the island. The consequence of all this is both considerable quantity and a strongly flavoured juice, almost imperceptibly salty and sulphurous in quality.

The wine produced is predominantly white, made either with the aromatic *athiri* grape (native of Rhodes) or the *asyrtiko* grape: a local variant of the latter is *Nychteri* wine, for which, as its name implies, the grapes are picked 'nocturnally' or rather in the early hours before the sun rises to a height sufficient to impart any heat. *Asyrtiko* mixed with *aidani* grapes are used for the production of the island's famed *Vin Santo*, whose name some believe derives from 'Santorini'. It is made by allowing the grapes, once picked, to reduce to sultanas by exposure to the sun, before vinification. The island's red wines are generally made with the tannic *mandilaria* grape, primarily associated with Paros. The habit of allowing the grapes to fortify and ferment on their own skins for a protracted period, producing a strong, dark, red wine or rosé-white wine, was introduced by the Venetians: this kind of wine traditionally bears the name *Brusco* on the island. The bottling of wine is a recent phenomenon in the Greek Islands, and it is still questionable to what extent wines such as those produced on Santorini benefit from bottling (even though it is required by the demands of marketing and uniformity). Much Greek wine should be drunk fresh from the barrel. It is increasingly hard to find this on Santorini, though one suggestion is made below under the 'Eating' section. Santorini sends some barrel-wine direct to particular locales in Athens: one of the best places to sample it is at the *Ouzeri Kouklis* in Tripodon Street in Plaka.

Beyond Megalochóri, the road turns east and heads for the south coast at Veríssa. To the left-hand side of the road, level with the village boundary sign of Emboreió, is the curious chapel of **Aghios Nikolaos *Marmaritis****, which is in effect an exceptionally well-preserved **marble shrine or temple of the 3rd century** BC, dedicated, according to an inscription still in situ, to the goddess Basíleia (*key held in the adjacent house*). This is an unusual place to find such a building; its size suggests that it may have functioned also as a family tomb.

The beautifully cut and laid, silver-grey limestone slabs of the walls have been partially cemented and re-pointed, but otherwise the building is a whole, ancient structure, complete with its marble roof supported by the original monolithic stone beams. The dimensions are diminutive (4.20m by 3.60m), with a dignified door frame in the south wall, and a small aedicule or niche on the inside of the north wall, framed by carved Ionic pilasters and a Doric entablature and pediment. The dedicatory inscription is engraved below. Basíleia is a curious divinity, whose cult is associated with that of Cybele, the mother goddess: she was the daughter of Uranus and Titaia, she married Hyperion (her brother), and was mother to Selene and Helios. Cult in the Hellenistic period is characterised by a restless search for new and ambiguous divinities, many of foreign origin.

Visible on the hill east of Aghios Nikolaos *Marmaritis* are the ruins of a four-square, **Venetian** *pyrgos*, known as a '*Goulas*' (from the Turkish *kule*, a tower). The design, which would suggest a construction date of the 16th century, is similar to those on Naxos, except that here, the heavy buttressing in the shape of a pronounced talus is strongly reminiscent of the Monastery of St John on Patmos and of its dependency on Naxos, the Monastery of Christos Fotodoti. The connection is further emphasised by the tradition that the tower had a chapel inside dedicated to the Blessed Christodoulos who founded St John on Patmos, and that it was at one time inhabited by Patmian monks. It was built as a fortified residence probably by the Venetian, d'Argenta family.

Emboreió* (sometimes Nimboreió; 8km) is the largest and most attractive of the island's inland villages. As often on Santorini, many of the oldest parts are built half-underground. In the midst of its tight tissue of passageways and streets are occasional sunken areas with a cluster of grotto-entrances and **troglodyte dwellings**. At the centre of the village is a **fortified** *kastro*, arranged around the **church of the Panaghia**. Near to it and beside the church of Aghios Charalambos are several ancient column fragments and *spolia*, suggesting that Emboreió could possibly occupy the site of the main settlement of Ancient *Eleusis*, whose cemetery lies, as we shall see, to the south of here, behind the port. The architecture of Emboreió is unusual and attractive; in contrast to the simple forms of the houses, the churches—especially the porticoes and belfries of the **church of Christós** and of the Panaghia—have an almost baroque insistence on tre-foil and multi-foil forms. Their belltowers are remarkable creations. Jean-Paul Sartre and Simone de Beauvoir visited Emboreió before the Second World War. Sartre later had the village in mind as the setting for his adaptation of the Electra legend, *Les Mouches* (1943).

The main road ends at the resort of **Períssa** (11km), which like Kamári stretches behind a beach of black, volcanic sand ending abruptly beneath the bulk of Mesa Vouno, this time on the south side. Scattered across the modern settlement near the foot of the mountain are several areas of excavation where remains of houses—thresholds and walls of the Roman and Hellenistic period—are being revealed. Behind the southeast corner of the dominating **church of the Tímios Stavrós** (Venerable Cross), sunk below the level of the church's surrounding patio, is the well-preserved base of a **marble funerary monument of the 1st century** AD in the form of a circular tower: each block has been meticulously faceted at the rim and the three existing courses of masonry stand on a finely moulded base-course. By the northeast corner of the same church are two standing columns of the same epoch. Between the church and the cliff are the ruins of the **Early Christian basilica of Aghia Irini**, after which the island took its name. It was probably founded in the 5th century, enlarged in the 6th century, abandoned, and then re-roofed in an improvised fashion in the 13th century. Its walls, and the large building to its northwest, incorporate material from pre-existing pagan structures.

The coastal road leads southwest to **Perívolos** and the harbour at **Vlycháda** (13km). The latter probably occupies the site of the southern outport of Ancient *Thera* during its final, Hellenistic phase (the port referred to by Claudius Ptolemy as *Eleusis*). An earthquake in 1570 has radically altered the coastline at this point, and it is not certain where the main settlement of ***Eleusis*** was situated. Its cemetery, however, has left many remains which can be seen to the north of the road between Perívolos and Vlycháda, in the rock of the cliff, always at a height of about three metres. Beginning at Perívolos and heading west, you encounter a series of **rock-cut tombs**, generally with steps below and pediments above, some framing conches and with decorated architectural elements. Leaving the road, for the track which hugs the foot of the bluff, you come to an isolated house, opposite which are several remains, including a couple of stepped platforms and **sarcophagi** carved out of the living rock and carefully shaped for the fitting of a lid. To the west of these, a path leads up through fallen masonry, towards a large **monumental tomb** above, with finely dressed, ashlar walls in two colours, framing the floor, threshold and steps, and a chamber beneath with a small entrance. These funerary monuments, some of distinction, probably date from the 2nd and 1st centuries BC, suggesting, in combination with the other remains in the area, that *Eleusis* prospered from the 3rd century BC, through into Early Christian times.

Until recently there were thermal springs at Vlycháda: the small barrel-vaulted bath-chamber can still be seen by the road to the west of the harbour.

AKROTIRI

From the junction (6km) on the main road between Megalochóri and Emboreió, a west branch leads to the **village of Akrotiri** (8.5km) and to the western extremity of the main island. The hill of Akrotiri is panoramic, and it was an obvious site for the Venetians to construct the fourth in their series of intercommunicating fortresses—this one watching the southern approaches to the island and its caldera. A branch of the Bolognese Gozzadini family, who were based on Siphnos and Kythnos, lived here already by 1336 and probably built the *kastro*; they were still occupying it in the 17th century under Turkish rule. Though ruined, the form of the ensemble survives well: the encircling ring of houses and quasi-bastions surround the summit, which was crowned originally by the main tower, whose ruins have been considerably modified to accommodate the modern church. The enceinte is entered by a tunnel above the church of Aghios Giorgios. Inside, there is a tightly-knit tissue of ruined buildings and the visible remains of plastered cisterns, and churches incorporating ancient fragments and *spolia*.

From Akrotiri, roads radiate west to the white bay and cliffs at Aspri, and beyond to the elegant **light-house** of Akrotiri point (13.5km), built by a French company in 1892, or south for the archaeological site, and the '**red beach**' which lies a short, fifteen-minute walk beyond it to the west.

The prehistoric site of Akrotiri
(N.B. Access to the excavations at Akrotiri has been closed by the Greek Public Prosecutor since a part of the metal roofing covering the archaeological site collapsed in September 2005 killing a tourist. Several dates, now passed, have been announced for the reopening: a realistic estimate is that the site should be open again from the 2011 season. The following description is of the site as it was at the time it closed.)

The excavations of the **prehistoric city at Akrotiri*** are among the most important in the Mediterranean because of the remarkably good state of conservation of the streets of two and three-storey buildings, the wealth of pottery and other finds, and the quality of the wall paintings, which constitute the most important cycle of Bronze Age murals in Europe. Some of the paintings are preserved in the Museum of Prehistoric Thera in Chora (*see above*), but most are in the National Archaeological Museum in Athens. For reasons of conservation, none have been kept on the site itself.

General observations on prehistoric Thera

Progress in excavation, because of the constant threat of collapse, has been slow. It is estimated that perhaps as little as one thirtieth of the overall extent of the site has been explored so far. No temple, or building dedicated *uniquely* to cult, has yet been discovered; nor any evidence of fortification or protective walls. In fact the often exceptionally broad windows of the houses so far uncovered suggest a kind of architecture which did not urgently take into consideration the possibility of external aggression. Any general observation about a site such as this will have to be modified continually as our knowledge is enhanced by the new discoveries being made; but we can begin by giving provisional impressions elicited by the nature of the settlement and its art, in comparison to others of the same or later periods:

- The considerable mercantile prosperity and high standard of living, with municipal services such as central drains and sewers beneath the streets, suggests a degree both of distribution of wealth within the society and of civic cooperation and social organisation amongst its various levels and elements.

- The wealth of imported objects, contrasted with the island's presumed paucity of exportable, home-grown agricultural goods, suggests that Bronze Age Therans were middle-men who lived off trade, commerce and shipping rather than production of primary materials: in other words, that the long-lasting Greek tradition of shipping as a major source of wealth goes back into this area's earliest history. As evidence of the importance of commercial exchange, it should be noted that half of the total number of examples of early stirrup-jars—the typical receptacle for transporting liquids such as wine or oil—in the Aegean area come from Akrotiri; similarly, two thirds of the balance-weights found in the Aegean also come from these excavations.

- From the unfortified architecture, the paucity of warrior's objects found, and the general lack of emphasis on martial themes in paintings, we may infer the non-aggressive nature of its society.

- Both the pottery decoration and the magnificently clear and vigorous wall paintings give a vivid sense of a confident, creative, civilised and, above all, colourful world, as different from the ponderous, martial world of the Mycenaeans on the one hand, as it was from the repetitive and protocol-bound world of Egypt on the other. The high proportion of empty space to figurative element in Theran painting is a deeply significant trait, revealing a freedom and clarity of thought. Evidence from the murex shells found, and from scenes of crocus picking depicted, suggest this was a world enlivened by purple and gold.

The excavations

Evidence of prehistoric settlement first came to light on Therasía in the 1860s, when a quarry which had been opened to provide *pozzolana* for the building of the Suez Canal, revealed a Bronze Age house of several rooms containing a wealth of pottery, which was briefly excavated by Ferdinand Fouqué in 1867. Fouqué also examined the site of Akrotiri, finding evidence of walls and strata composed of vase fragments. As a consequence of his finds, a team from the French School of Archaeology under Henri Mamet, dug at Akrotiri in 1870, and published their findings (in Latin) four years later. Following a brief campaign of excavation, to the east of the present site, by Robert Zahn in 1899, nothing further was done for almost seventy years. In 1939 Spyros Marinatos published an article suggesting that the destruction of Knossos and of Cretan civilisation was the result of violent volcanic activity on Thera. It was not until 1967 that he first began digging at Akrotiri, having surveyed the whole area a few years previously. By a combination of good luck and brilliant foresight, he made significant finds from the very first days of excavation, when he descended into a room with a large window, containing decorated and painted storage vases. Marinatos died on the site as the result of an accident while excavating in 1974. Since then, the excavations have continued under the guidance of Professor Christos Doumas. Several thousand tons of volcanic ash and pumice have been removed from an area of about 2 hectares, but the excavations are still in their infancy.

History of the settlement

Evidence from pottery finds shows that the site of Akrotiri was inhabited since the late Neolithic period (5th millennium BC), that it grew through the early 3rd millennium BC (Early Cycladic period), and that it became a flourishing settlement in the Middle Cycladic period. On exceptionally clear days, the mountains of Crete are visible from parts of Thera, and Akrotiri is the point on the island closest to Crete. It is the very first landfall for maritime traffic heading north from Crete. Links between the two islands must have been close from the Middle Cycladic period on, and some scholars have suggested that the settlement at Akrotiri was a Minoan trading colony. The truth is more complex: although there is clearly strong Minoan influence, there are many elements of architecture, town planning, painting and ceramic production which betray a quite independent Cycladic parentage. What is visible to the visitor today, therefore, is a town of the mid-17th century BC, which is a hybrid of Minoan and Cycladic features. Several times in its history the town was destroyed or damaged by earthquakes; on each occasion the ruins were levelled, and new building was begun above, following the same urban plan. This meant that the street level rose, and at several points ground floor rooms became half-sunken basements. In the seismic events leading up to the final eruption of Thera, the town was evacuated more than once and then re-occupied in moments of quiescence, in which repairs to the damaged buildings were undertaken. Before the final cataclysm it appears that the population had sufficient warning to collect their valuable belongings and animals, and to leave. In contradistinction to Pompeii and Herculaneum, no bodies and few real valuables have been found in excavations so far. After the final eruption in c. 1625 BC, the town was buried and preserved by the packed and hardened volcanic ash.

The architecture and paintings

The state of preservation of the buildings is remarkable with many standing to two floors, some to three. A good proportion of the houses were built of loose stone with a mud and straw mortar. To give them both strength and flexibility during earth tremors they had large wooden frames to the windows and doors, sometimes reinforced with cut, stone blocks around the frame and at the corners of the buildings. These wooden elements were incinerated by the heat of the volcanic ash which packed around them: this has meant that the archaeologists have had to proceed with extreme caution to avoid the collapse of the buildings. The negative space left by every wooden element has had to be filled with a cement before the internal spaces could be cleared. What look like wooden beams in the houses, are in fact the cement beams of the archaeologists. In places, too, buttresses have had to be added. Alongside the houses in this adobe construction, are a number of large, possibly public, edifices constructed entirely or partially in ashlar masonry, i.e. dry-stone masonry of regularly cut blocks. The two large buildings to either side of the south entrance to the site, designated *Xeste 3* and *Xeste 4* are examples, the former being a two-storey block with 14 rooms on each floor. (*Xeste* in Greek refers to a building of large-cut stone blocks.) Staircases were generally in stone, and sometimes in wood. The roofs were flat and thermally insulated, comprising cross-beams overlaid with reeds and branches packed and sealed with earth and crushed shells, in a fashion almost identical to traditional Cycladic structures existing today. Floors were constructed similarly and, in more important residences, they were paved with schist slabs. The lowest, semi-basement floors were cool and used for storage, or as workshops: rows of *pithoi* were commonly found at this level. The upper floor was for reception rooms; their walls were coated with a fine plaster, often coloured or painted, and the most common object they contained was a loom, suggesting that they were predominantly women's quarters. Privies, with a bench-seat, connected by down-pipes to a communal drain that ran under the paving of the street outside, are found in some houses, for example in Room 4 of the West House (*see p. 85*). Perhaps the most remarkable feature of these houses was the unusual size of their broad, open windows, through which it must have been possible sometimes to see the colourful wall paintings within, from the public spaces outside. These paintings constitute Akrotiri's greatest gift to our understanding of the Aegean Bronze Age world (*see panel above*).

Tour of the site

The excavations occupy a long hollow which runs along a north/south axis. Entry to the site is generally at the south (lower) end, into an open space between two large building complexes to left and to right. **Xeste 3**, to the left, appears to have been a two-floored dwelling with many rooms and a sacred area, constructed in ashlar masonry. The rooms in the part nearest to us were decorated with paintings, and must have functioned as an *adyton*, or place of cult. The paintings, depicting the *Crocus Gatherers*, covered both lower and upper floors; they featured women gathering wild crocus and putting them into baskets to offer them to a seated female divinity, flanked by a monkey and a gryphon. **Xeste 4**, to the right, which is an extensive three-floor building, is currently under excavation and has revealed interesting decorations, amongst which is a depiction of a boar-tusk helmet, of a kind similar to that described by Homer. As the open area closes into a small alley to the north, it passes the two-floor **Building B** (*left*): this was again magnificently decorated with the famous images of *Antelopes* and *Boxing Children*, in which the adjacent images of young, male competition in the human and animal worlds, provided a deliberate iconographic symmetry. A small room on the western side of the same building was decorated with the scene of scrambling *Blue Monkeys*, which is on display in the Museum of Prehistoric Thera in Chora (*see p. 31*). In **Building D**, further north to the left, the large door and window frames, and **storage areas with *pithoi***, can be clearly seen as they were found. At this point the municipal **drainage system** runs beneath the level of the pathway, the built-in down-pipes can also be seen at certain points. An example of a Minoan type of altar in the form of ox-horns, referred to as 'Horns of Consecration', is exhibited near to where it was found to the right-hand side, underlining the close cultic links with Crete. As the street climbs further, a flight of partially collapsed stone steps to an upper floor can be seen to the left. You are now above the area of the cemetery of the earlier, 3rd millennium BC settlement. Respect was paid by the later inhabitants to the sacredness of this spot by the preservation of a small stone **cenotaph** (*to the left*) which contained marble figurines and grave goods from the cemetery, and which was always left visible in the city. Further to the north and slightly to the left, at the summit, (*currently not accessible*) is the so-called **House of the Ladies**, named after the murals (now in the Museum of Prehistoric Thera in Chora; *see p. 29*) depicting elegant ladies in flounced dresses, participating in what appears to be a ritual dressing of a priestess or important female person. At the northern extremity of the site is the **Building of the *Pithoi***, where a concentration of variously decorated, standing storage jars were found in a room with a large, low window perhaps used for dispensing the produce. It was here that Spyros Marinatos made his first sounding on the site in 1967.

The permitted route leads round to the west (*left*) and down a narrow alley into the small and intimate **Triangle Square*** dominated to the north by the most important building excavated so far, the **West House**. With little effort we can imagine ourselves in the *plateia* of a contemporary Cycladic town—something that shows how practical and enduring the design of settlements has been, with narrow, curving streets and small, open areas to break the force of the frequent winds. The West House presents an interesting façade: the low window-lights, just above the ground level, are sufficient to supply ventilation and light for the cool, lower-floor storage areas. At the right-hand end is an entrance doorway with a rectangular window directly beside it: this is a common feature of houses at Akrotiri, and is notably similar to the design of shopfronts in Pompeii and Herculaneum. The upper floor is dominated by the central, rectangular window, behind which is a large, ceremonial room; to its west are two rooms which were beautifully decorated. The murals which came from here and occupied almost every kind and shape of space, all partake of a marine theme: the two *Fisher-boys Bearing Strings of Fish* marched from opposite corners to a meeting point where the small, three-legged offering table, decorated with dolphins (in the Museum of Prehistoric Thera in Chora; *see p. 29*) was found by Marinatos. Above were a series of friezes depicting *Marine and River Landscapes* and a more detailed scene of what appears to have been a *Naval Regatta* which, even if we are unable fully to understand the nature of the event it depicts, provides through its extraordinary detail invaluable information on costume, architecture, boat design and fauna. These constitute the earliest 'landscapes' in European Art. Another imposing house, **Building D**, forms the east side of the little *plateia*. It was from a small room on the far side of this house that the most bucolic of all the Theran paintings comes: the colourful *Landscape with Lilies and Swallows* (Archaeology Museum, Athens) which formed the backdrop to a ritual, celebrating the returning fertility of spring. The house had a grand entrance which was covered with a roofed porch, open to north and south, which encroaches on the public space, just to the south of the square. It was in the building beyond this that Spyros Marinatos died while working on the excavations in October 1974. A small memorial inside the building marks the spot.

THERASIA

Notwithstanding its proximity (2km) to one of the most popular tourist destinations in Europe, Therasía has remained remarkably quiet and untouched. A visit to the island is a return in time: it gives some sense of what Santorini was like before tourism transformed it. The landscape is similar, but empty except for the pasturing animals—horses, donkeys and the mules which winter on Therasía after their summer's exertions on the main island carrying visitors from the port up to Firá. The vegetation and birdlife is richer than on Santorini: larks fill the air in spring, with raptors circling above them. Fruit-cactus and capers are abundant. The plentiful vines on Therasía are mostly of the white *Kritikó* grape.

On the scarp above the waterfront at **Ríva**, is the mid-19th-century **church of Aghia Irini**, sitting in a wide esplanade. An ancient column fragment outside the church is the sole reminder of an ancient presence in the area which it seems most likely would have occupied the spur of the hill to the south of Ríva, where there is a density of terracing and walls. The two hamlets on the gentler, western slope of the island make a rewarding visit. Both **Potamós** and **Agriliá** (*30mins by foot from Ríva*) are hidden in ravines in the island's western slope, giving them a compact and intimate feel. In Potamós, the rows of house-fronts belonging to the older dwellings carved deep into the rock form a variegated backdrop to the later dwellings in front which are vaulted and cubic in design. Plants burgeon in the ravine's meagre water. In Agriliá, the **church of the Panaghia ton Eisodion** (Presentation of the Virgin), built in 1887, has striking and colourful folkloric decoration on its façade, of a kind not seen on the main island.

Manólas (*40mins by foot from Ríva*), the island's *chora*, beetles along the eastern ridge of the island at 170m above sea level, mirroring Firá opposite, across the caldera. A steep crescent bay drops below to **Kórfos**, the island's primary harbour, lined with old vaulted boathouses and fisherman's dwellings. Manólas preserves much of its original patchwork of troglodyte houses whose doors and windows and projecting ovens create fascinating patterns in the flows and bulges of the natural pumice-rock. Most of the village's churches were rebuilt after the earthquake of 1956. Some, such as the tiny chapel of **Aghios Ioannis Prodromos** with its prominent belfries, are a delight for the ingenuous gaiety of their decoration.

To the south of Manólas the track along the ridge leads past several rural churches built in small, fertile hollows

to the monastery of the **Koimisis tis Theotokou**, pano-
ramically sited on the southernmost point of the island,
200m above the water. In the southwest corner of the island, south of the church of Christós, are the **Alaphouzos**
***pozzolana* quarries**, whose pumice was used in the prep-
aration of a vitally important, impermeable cement for
the construction of the Suez Canal. In 1866 a Greek sci-
entist, Manolis Christomanos, observed man-made walls
at the lower limit of the quarry and saw that they were
pre-Greek, dating from before the pumice layers above
were deposited. Alaphouzos, the proprietor of the quarry
organised excavation of the site, from which a house with
several rooms was uncovered, with associated pottery.
Fouqué also studied the site. This was the first intimation of the prehistoric importance of *Thera*, which was
to lead eventually to Marinatos's spectacular discoveries
at Akrotiri.

CHRISTIANA

Twenty kilometres southeast of Santorini, and clearly visible in good weather conditions, is the steep and uninhabited island of Christiana—Ancient *Ascania*. Evidence
of a settlement of the 3rd millennium BC has come to
light on the island, including a cylindrical, underground

construction in the form of a well, carefully lined in dry stone. The island is remote and difficult of access: the early human presence there raises interesting questions about sea-craft and sailing skills in the Early Bronze Age, a subject about which we know lamentably little.

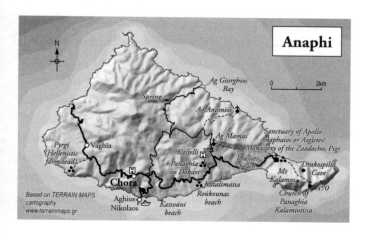

ANAPHI

'*... there exists no island so remote in its solitude as Anaphi,*'
wrote Theodore Bent after his visit in January of 1883. '*It
is a mere speck in the waves, in the direction of Rhodes or
Crete, where no one ever goes, and where the 1,000 inhabitants of the one village thereon are as isolated as if they dwelt
in an archipelago in the Pacific.*'

Anaphi is the most arid of the inhabited islands in the
Aegean: precipitous, rocky, and virtually harbourless,
but with an unforgettable and dramatic profile when
seen from the sea or from neighbouring Santorini. At
its eastern end the great rock promontory of Kalamos,
rises sheer from the sea almost half a kilometre upwards
into the air. In spring, its top is often circled with clouds:
when they part, the tiny silhouette of the church of the
Panaghia Kalamiotissa can be seen against the sky, sus-
pended above the precipice. At the foot of the mountain
is the sanctuary of Apollo *Aigletes*, whose cult is believed
to have been first instituted here by Jason and the Argonauts. It is a remarkable ruin, with the walls of the temple
in honey-coloured marble, standing between three and
four metres high, and the ramparts of the massive terrace

of the precinct visible on all sides—an unexpected sight on such a small and remote island. The interest of Anaphi lies in its surprises: in the fields on the open hillside of Kastelli, beside the chapel of the Panaghia sto Dokari, a finely decorated Roman sarcophagus has survived almost intact from the cemetery of Ancient *Anaphe*, whose ruins lie waiting to be excavated. Until a few years ago, full-size funerary statues could also be seen lying in the undergrowth in the area. They have now been moved under cover for their protection.

The accessibility of such a wealth of antiquities is part of Anaphi's unfussy simplicity, and its remoteness. Santorini, its closest neighbour, is three hours away by an often erratic ferry service; and its pace of life is many worlds away. Anaphi feels like a forgotten frontier, and that constitutes the basis of its appeal. The island has unblemished, south-facing, sandy beaches, and wild valleys in its interior, dotted with ancient and traditional stone farmsteads; but, both inland and at the shore, the island is rigorously treeless. Its beauty is rugged in the best and hardest sense, like the character of its islanders.

HISTORY AND LEGEND

According to one tradition, Anaphi was first settled at the same time as *Thera* by Phoenicians in the company of Membliaros, companion of Cadmus, and was named *Bliaros*. According to Apollonius of Rhodes, its name (cognate with the Greek word, ἀναφαίνειν', 'to make apparent') derives from the moment when Apollo revealed the island to Jason and his fellow Argonauts in a flash of lightning during a storm which threatened their lives, thereby offering them safe haven (Apollonius Rhodius, *Argonautica, IV, 1694–1730*). Others suggest the name is a crasis of two words ἄνευ' and ὄφις', implying that the island was 'without snakes'; their absence is commented on by Theodore Bent. Other antique sources refer to the quantity of partridge on the island. Like Ancient *Thera*, *Anaphe* was a Dorian colony of the 9th or 8th century BC. In the 5th century BC it was assessed to pay a tribute of 1,000 *drachmae* into the Athenian League. The island seems to have reached a peak of prosperity, with many new impressive buildings in the 4th century BC; in the same period, it also began minting its own coins, bearing the head of Apollo on the obverse, and a *krater* with a bee on the reverse. This prosperity was perhaps not unrelated to the proximity and increased influence of Ancient *Thera*.

The island, later known as 'Nanfio', was given by Marco Sanudo to his comrade in arms, Leonardo Foscolo, in 1207 at the time of the establishment of the Duchy of Naxos. In 1269, a local privateer, Giovanni della Cava, commanding a detachment of the Byzantine fleet, captured and held it until 1307, when it once again returned to Venetian control, this time under Gianuli Gozzadini, who subsequently controlled it as a fief of Nicolo I Sanudo in Naxos. In 1480 the island passed as a marriage dowry to Domenico Pisani, whose family held the island until it was sacked by Khaireddin Barbarossa in the winter of 1537/8. From 1540 Anaphi was formalised as an Ottoman possession, which it remained until the Greek War of Independence, apart from a brief interval between 1770–74, when it was taken by Count Alexei Orloff during the First Russo-Turkish War. During the Russian occupation, many of the island's antiquities were removed to St Petersburg. In 1821, Anaphi contributed two boats and crews to the cause of Greek Independence, and in 1832, the island was assumed into the Greek State. Such a large number of islanders emi-

grated during the 19th century to Athens that the picturesque quarter of Plaka below the east face of the Acropolis,
around the church of Aghios Giorgios 'tou Vrachou', is to
this day called *Anaphiótika*. The area still possesses the feel
of an island *chora*. Many of the émigrés were craftsmen
who worked on the building of the Royal Palace. During
the military dictatorships of the last century Anaphi was
used as a detention centre for political exiles.

ANAPHI CHORA

The tranquil and uneventful **Chora** of Anaphi clusters
around the remains of the medieval, Venetian castle on
the crest of a hill almost 300m above the landing jetty
at Aghios Nikolaos, in the middle of the south coast of
the island. The main settlement of the island in antiquity
lay several kilometres to the east; this new site must have
been chosen by the Venetians because of the sharp outcrop of rock on the hill top—marked today by the chapel
of Aghios Giorgios—which provided an easily fortifiable
and strategic point. The *kastro*, of which only meagre
remains survive, dates from the 15th century, when the
island had passed from the stewardship of the Sanudo to

the Crispo family. Some of the houses in the steep alleys near the summit, must be only a little more recent. The settlement winds in a crescent towards a small *plateia* at the western end of the village passing the settlement's principal, early 17th-century **church of Aghios Nikolaos**.

The village today is an attractive and airy settlement: its appearance is characterised by countless, half-cylindrical vaults over **traditional single-room dwellings**, whose forms alternate with the round, masonry ovens—like truncated towers with low roofs—which stand close to the entrance of each house. The base of the vaulted roofs was surrounded by a low rim which caught rainwater, channelling it into cisterns below. The modern buildings which have accreted to this historic core have mostly followed the same architectural characteristics, but on a larger scale. On the east slope of the *kastro*, directly behind the *Koinótita* (Municipality) building is the temporary seat of the **Archaeological Collection** (*for access, ask in the Municipality offices*).

Although currently no more than a small stack-room, this contains a magnificent selection of **Roman funerary statues**. All lack their heads; the busts are heavily draped with the drill-cut folds of togas, partially covering the hands which are positioned in some cases so as to hold the material over the head in a sign of mourning. Such busts would originally have been produced in series and left unfinished until the time of purchase, at which point the separate head with the appropriate personalised features of the face was fitted onto the bust. These pieces come from the necropolis on the southeastern slope of Kastelli Hill, where until recently they were lying exposed on the hillside. There are also several Early Christian inscriptions in the collection. Anaphi's greatest treasure, the very fine, late 6th-century BC *Anaphe Kouros*, known as the Strangford Apollo, is now in the British Museum, London.

East from Chora: Kastelli Hill

The principal interest of the island lies to the east of Chora, accessible by a road which follows the coast at a short distance inland. The landscape is rigorously Cycladic—treeless, and rocky, with bald hillsides, a few of which were once laboriously terraced over their entire extent. The thick cover of herbs at ground level supports a good bee population; the island was celebrated for its honey in antiquity—even featuring the image of a bee on its coinage—and still produces honey of good quality. The most conspicuous plant of all is the fruit-cactus which alone has the possibility to flourish here, especially in the protected enclosures of the ruined buildings. At the shore, along this southeast sector of the coast, are the island's best beaches—**Katsoúni**, **Flamouroú**, **Roúkounas** and **Prassiés**—which have impressive sweeps of sand, but little shade. In summer, small boats from the harbour provide the simplest way of reaching them.

At c. 4km from Chora the road begins to traverse the southern slope of the hill of Kastelli. The summit to the north was the acropolis of Ancient *Anaphe*, now crowned with the remains of Venetian fortification; below stretched the area of habitation. To the south by the shore was the city's port, grouped around the bay of Katalymákia, or **Katalymátsa**, whose name derives from the ancient Greek words for an inn or hostel. The area visible on the undulating land above the shore, a few minutes' walk below the road, is marked by a large number of curious, stone cairns which are said to have been raised by local mariners who traditionally added a stone when departing for a journey: the inlet here was formerly the island's harbour. The soft earth consists of a high proportion of volcanic deposit from Santorini. Although most of the surface finds were taken from here in the 18th century by the Russian occupiers during the First Russo-Turkish War, there are still remains lying all around, and the area in general is asking for excavation. On the sharp rise to the north side are many **classical *spolia***: fragments of capital and architrave and fluted column. In the middle of the rear ridge is a small chapel, constructed from many large pieces of ancient masonry, and with an upturned capital serving as a table by the door. A ridge, marked by the mariners' cairns (partially consisting of antique fragments), runs west from here to a point where there is a clear view of the ancient harbour-inlet, with the sweep of what were once terraced habitations behind. Amongst their remains are **blocks of architrave** in marble from Naxos or Paros, and an eroded, **carved *stele*** still standing. The extent of the site suggests that the main concentration of the population of **Ancient *Anaphe*** may latterly have been here by the port. The presence of some discarded marble elements which have been (re-)cut for use in a church *templon*, indicates that the site also continued to be used into Christian times.

As the road momentarily climbs inland, a footpath leads left up the adjacent slope of the hillside towards the summit of **Kastelli**, and to the interesting **church of the Panaghia sto Dokari**, which is gained in about ten minutes. The north side of the church is buttressed on the outside by a segment of **ancient retaining wall** in large, regular limestone blocks; the goat-byre a short distance to the southeast of the church similarly has its rear wall (visible from inside) composed of the same massive elements. The general construction of the blocks is of a kind that would suggest 4th-century BC work, although the size and shape of the elements may indicate an earlier period; what exactly this configuration of walls formed is hard to ascertain from the scant evidence. The most notable remnant, is the beautifully decorated, marble **Roman sarcophagus*** beside the church, which stands complete with its broken lid carved as if with roof-tiles. There are **eroded reliefs** on all four sides: a scene of dancing *putti* and of gryphons on the long sides, and of a Siren and of (?) *Alexander Taming Bellerophon* on the short sides. The footpath, though faint, continues to the summit of the hill (325m above sea level) where a network of walls remain from the ample medieval, **Venetian fortress**, built around the panoramic outcrop of rock on the summit which had functioned since earliest antiquity as the ancient acropolis. Leonardo Foscolo, in the 13th century, probably established his first abode on the island here, before the founding of Chora. The medieval walls incorporate many ancient blocks, and there are the remains of the base of an ancient temple.

From the summit of Kastelli, the path descends and crosses a saddle to the north east, and then makes for the church of Aghios Mámas, where there are further ruins of late Hellenistic and Roman **tombs**, some with sunken chambers. From Aghios Mámas a ninety-minute walk leads first northwest to the rural settlement of Aghios Dimitrios, and thence east to the **monastery of Aghios Antonios at Kastraki**, which is said to have the remains of 14th-century paintings in its interior. The main path from Aghios Mámas, however, continues east along the south slope of Mount Chalépas, following the line of the **Sacred Way** that joined the ancient city to the Sanctuary of Apollo on the eastern isthmus of the island: parts of its paved surface are clearly visible in stretches. The path ends at the isthmus after one and a half hours from Katalymátsa, or two hours from Chora.

The metalled road meanwhile continues from Katalymátsa to Mégas Potamós (6km), a ravine with small spots of cultivation, and thence down to the shore at the solitary **chapel of the Aghii Anárgyri** (7km). The altar inside is supported by a small Corinthian capital, and other ancient fragments have been collected outside. The road ends (8km) at the monastery on the isthmus, where it is joined by the footpath (*see above*) from Kastelli, via Aghios Mámas.

THE SANCTUARY OF APOLLO '*AIGLETES*' AND THE MONASTERY OF THE ZOODOCHOS PIGI

The monastery of the Panaghia Kalamiótissa, dedicated to the Zoödochos Pigi or Virgin as Life-giving Source, which stands on the ridge of the neck of land joining the dramatic rock of Kalamos to the island, has become once again home to nine monks after a recent period of abandonment. It occupies the site of the ancient **Sanctuary of Apollo *Anaphaios* or *Aigletes****, one of the most singular and interesting in the Cyclades. There are impressive remains of the **temple** and its **sacred precinct**, standing to a considerable height; many of the marble blocks also preserve clear inscriptions.

Origins of the cult

The legendary origins of the sanctuary are very ancient: it is said to have been founded by Jason and the Argonauts in gratitude to Apollo who saved them from a terrible storm. Jason in desperation besought Apollo to appear and to help them. Apollonius (*Argonautica, IV, 1694 ff.*) relates it thus:

> *Then, [Apollo] son of Leto, quick to hear, you descended from heaven to the Melantian islets lying in the sea.*

Then alighting on one of the twin peaks, you raised up your golden bow with your right hand; and the bow flashed a dazzling light all about. And before [the Argonauts] appeared a small island of the Sporades, opposite tiny Hippouris, and there they cast anchor and stayed.

The *Melantioi Petrai* are the two humped islets visible to the southeast of the island, and *Hippouris* the reef between them and Anaphi. The burst of light, 'αἴγλη', gives the divinity here the epithet *Aigletes*; and the name of the island derives from 'ἀναφαίνειν', to 'bring to light' or 'make apparent', both associations with the Jason legend. Apollonius adds that the Argonauts had nothing more than water to sacrifice to the god: as they did this, the Phaeacian servant-women who accompanied them, laughed at their actions, eliciting a friendly exchange of jokes and taunts between the men and women. It thereafter became a tradition on the island to stage a trading of insults and jokes whenever they sacrificed to Apollo *Aigletes*.

The buildings

The marble used here, which is of local origin, has unusual characteristics: it has a high quartz content which causes it to glint and catch the light, but which also makes it subject to corrosion by salt, as can be seen on the north side of the sanctuary retaining wall. Around the entrance are fluted column fragments and other architectural elements. To the right-hand side of the doorway an excellently preserved stretch of wall, in courses of beautifully cut marble, snugly fitted over the irregular rock outcrops on the surface, rises over three metres high: this is **the west wall of the main temple's *naos***. The masonry dates the construction to the 4th century BC. To either side of the entrance are two blocks carved with **ancient inscriptions** in fine Hellenistic lettering, amongst many later, modern graffiti; there are other ancient inscriptions just beyond.

To the right on entering is the **enclosed *naos*** of the temple, constructed in regular blocks of honey-veined marble. Walls of such height and preservation are a rare and beautiful sight. The design is unusual: the ancient building would appear to have been *prostyle* in plan, with a porch only on the front. This led into a ***pronaos***, which was curiously divided into two enclosed rooms to either side of the entrance. A door, whose architrave-block bears a long Hellenistic **inscription**, then led from the *pronaos* into the *naos*. The former refectory of the monastery, now disused, was built inside it. The present *catholicon* of the monastery, standing to the east, is modern, but it is built on ancient foundations, a couple of courses of which survive. Extending to the east and north of the monastery enclosure are the ponderous walls built up from below to support the **platform of the sanctuary**, their corners meticulously drafted, as always. The presence of several other stylobates of buildings indicate that there were altars and temples to other deities within the same precinct: inscriptions refer to the cult also of Artemis, Aphrodite, Asklepios and of Zeus *Ktesios*. For so small an island this was an important sanctuary. The prevalence of Hellenistic building suggests that the island enjoyed particular prosperity in this period, probably in conjunction with the Ptolemaic presence at Ancient *Thera*, directly across the water to the west.

The temples would have looked out east over Chalara Bay, where two spikes of strikingly green rock rise from the sea, indicating a presence of iron ore.

From the monastery, it is a seventy five-minute climb by an often precipitous path up to the summit of the **Kalamos rock**, at 460m. This imposing natural phenomenon rises almost sheer on its south face, and only marginally more gently to the north, giving it the form of a wave, moving south, about to break: the effect is enhanced by the spumes of cloud that often strafe its summit. Low down on its north slope is the **Drakospiliá**, a large cave with stalactite formations. In a rock eyrie, a short distance below and west of the summit, sits the **church of the Panaghia Pano Kalamiótissa,** called [A]pano to distinguish it from the monastery (Kato) below. This courageous site, frequently in the full force of the wind, was a small monastic dependency, now abandoned, centred on the 18th-century church which is built out on a ledge. It may well occupy the site of a pagan shrine. The **view*** reputedly encompasses the mountains of Crete on a clear day.

West of Chora

The dry landscape to the west of Chora appears capable of sustaining only breaks of prickly-pear in the creases where water accumulates. But the many traditional, rural dwellings (now mostly abandoned) suggest that the land has rendered a living for generations through animal husbandry and a limited cultivation of grain. The stone farmstead, or **katoikía**, is a particular feature of the Anaphi landscape, and is different from those on other Cycladic islands. It generally comprises several buildings, grouped beside a threshing floor: a small dwelling, an oven, animal pens, a storage barn etc. The low rectangular profile is always broken by the surprisingly large **baking-ovens** which rise above the roof-level like truncated cones. The roofs of the buildings are flat: the rafters are covered with canes, packed and sealed with seaweed and mud, and then covered with a scattering of small, flat stones.

After Kaméni Langáda (2.5km), the road west of Chora rises sharply to a curve where it levels out with wide views: due south, above the coast, is visible a long, low *katoikía*, about twenty five minutes by foot from the road. This is **Pyrgí**, where the main body of the building complex is formed by the massive base of a **Hellenistic farmstead** measuring about nine and a half metres square, built up in courses of irregular rectangular blocks of the native stone. Although the position is panoramic, with Mount Prophitis Elias on Santorini clearly visible in front, the lack of fallen masonry would suggest that this was never a higher structure or watchtower, but a principally agricultural building protecting and surveying the cultivated uplands of the west of the island. This area may have been much more fertile in antiquity. Today the only outbreak of fertility is at **Vághia** (3.5km), where a spring has unexpectedly fostered stands of reeds and a small, vivid band of cultivation.

PRACTICAL INFORMATION

847 00-02 **Santorini:** area 76 sq. km; perimeter 67km; resident population 13,447; maximum altitude 567m. **Port Authority:** T: 22860 22239 **Travel information:** Pelican Travel (T: 22860 22220; www.pelican.gr) **General information:** www.santorini.com

840 09 **Anafi or Anaphi:** area 38 sq. km; perimeter 38km; resident population 272; maximum altitude 579m. **Port Authority:** T: 22860 61216 **Travel information:** T: 22860 61408 or from Zeyzed Travel (T: 22860 61253) **General information:** www.anafi.gr

ACCESS

By air: Santorini is well-connected with four daily flights to Athens with both Olympic Air and Aegean Airlines, and three to Thessaloniki with Aegean. Aegean also operate a once-weekly direct flight to and from Milan and Rome, from July to September. The airport takes large aircraft, and is four and a half kilometres from Chora.
By boat: At **Santorini** the (new) ferry port (Athiniós) is seven and a half kilometres from Chora. There are generally two or

three daily boat connections to Piraeus, taking nine hours by car-ferry and five hours by high-speed vessel; most stop at Paros and/or Naxos en route. There are links to Anaphi, Folegandros, Sikinos and Ios, and with Crete, five or six times weekly (these drop to twice-weekly in the winter). There are direct links to Milos twice-weekly throughout the year. Boats for **Therasía** leave from the port of Oia at Amoudi (12km from Chora), daily at 8am and midday, to Ríva. A connecting local bus to Potamós and Manólas (Chora)—10 mins. Sometimes the boat route includes Kórfos harbour, directly below Manólas, in addition to Ríva. **Anaphi** is at the end of the line for two ferry routes from Athens: F/B *Panaghia Tinou*, which leaves Lavrion for Anaphi twice-weekly, via Syros, Naxos and Santorini, with stops at the lesser islands en route; and F/B *Romilda* which leaves from Piraeus twice-weekly stopping at the same islands. F/B Arsinoe connects Anaphi with Santorini three times weekly. The island has no taxi.

LODGING

On **Santorini**, the **Kavalari Hotel** (*T: 22860 22347, fax 22603, www.kavalari.com*) is one of the older hotels on the island, centrally placed, with magnificent views, created from traditional Santorinian houses cut into the native lava at the top of the cliff above the caldera. It is simple, friendly, unpretentious, and beautiful: there is no elevator, however, and the rooms are reached down precipitous flights of steps. For greater ease of access (also near the Metropolitan Church) is the **Theoxenia Hotel** (*T: 22860 22740, fax 22950, www.theoxenia.net*): panoramic and very pleasant, with a good breakfast served in the rooms. The island's oldest hotel, **The Atlantis** (*T: 22860 22111, fax 22821, www.atlantishotel.gr*) is practical, straightforward, welcoming and superbly sited; it is one of the few hotels open all year

round. The **Aressana Hotel** (*T: 22860 22860, fax 23902, www.aressana.gr*), opposite the Atlantis, is also comfortably appointed and convenient. On one of the highest points of the cliff, with views directly over the caldera, **Anteliz Apartments Hotel** (*T: 22860 28842, fax 28843, www.anteliz.gr*) is modern and attractive, with spacious rooms and a pool. For 'boutique chic', **Homeric Poems** (*T: 22860 24661, fax 24660, www.homericpoems.gr*) offers a luxurious and rarified atmosphere.

Oia is generally more tranquil than Chora; it also has the most delightful place to stay on the island—**Chelidonia Villas** (*T: 22860 71827, fax 71649,* *www.chelidonia.com*), which combines simplicity with good taste, friendliness and a perfect position.

On **Therasía** there are rooms to rent at **Zacharo**, just above Manólas to the south, T: 22860 29102.

Lodging is not plentiful on **Anaphi**. The most comfortable option on the island is **Villa Apollon** (*T: 22860 61348; www.apollonvilla.gr*), overlooking Kleisidi Bay, not far from the harbour. **Ta Plagia** (*T: 22860 61308; www.taplagia.gr*) in Chora offers pleasant and panoramic, self-catering studios. A complete list of rooms available for rent in Chora can be found on www.anaphi.gr.

EATING

Between the twin traps of the expensively pretentious and the indifferently touristic, there are still a few good places to eat on **Santorini**. **Ta Delphinia** at the water's edge in the Bay of Akrotiri is a family-run fish taverna, which largely serves its own catch of fish accompanied by its own local wine (from March to August), and an array of traditional *mezés*, which include a delicious Santorinian fava and *tomatokeftedes*. The taverna **Aktaion** (often known as 'Roussos') at the very beginning of Firostefáni (coming by foot from Chora), though small, serves local food, including a good *prassopitta*—a pie made with mixed greens and leeks. 50m north of it, is the best and most genuine Italian eatery in the Aegean (run by Italians), called **Il Cantuccio**. For a more highly-wrought cuisine, still based on Greek ingredients, **Selene** at the southern extremity of Chora offers peace and a beautiful view in addition to some interesting dishes. **Franco's Bar** in Chora merits mention as a historic institution: one of the first bars of the 1970s on Santorini, it still serves (expensive, but well-prepared) cocktails to the accompaniment of classical music, in front of one of the most dramatic sunsets in Europe.

On **Therasía**, **Taverna Panórama** in Manólas, at the top of the steps from the harbour of Kórfos, has an excellent view, passable food, but wayward prices.

On **Anaphi**, **To Steki** in Chora is lively and welcoming, with a good selection of salads and meats. For fish, **Liotrivi Café** is perhaps a slightly better option.

FURTHER READING

Santorini
Ferdinand Fouqué, whose book *Santorini et Ses Eruptions* was first published in French in 1879, and reissued in an English translation by Alexander McBirney in 1999 by Johns Hopkins University Press, is the first comprehen-

sive study of the island's geology and volcanic history. **J.V. Luce**, *The End of Atlantis* (first published by Thames & Hudson, London, 1969; reprinted by Efstathiadis & Sons, Athens, 1982) is indebted to Fouqué, but follows the theme of Plato's legend of Atlantis and its relation to Santorini. **Nanno Marinatos**, in *Art & Religion in Thera: Reconstructing a Bronze Age Society* (Athens, 1984) lays out a clear and cogent explanation of the paintings from Akrotiri. *The Wall Paintings of Thera* (Athens, 1992) by **Christos Doumas**, the current head of excavations at Akrotiri, is also authoritative and clear on the subject—as are all his many excellent articles and writings on Theran matters.

Anaphi

Theodore Bent's description of his visit to Anaphi in 1883 is one of the most succinct and informative chapters in his account, *The Cyclades, or Life among the Insular Greeks* (1885: reissued 2002 by Archaeopress, Oxford in the 3rd Guides series). It gives a vivid account of the isolated life of Anaphi's (then) one thousand inhabitants.

INDEX

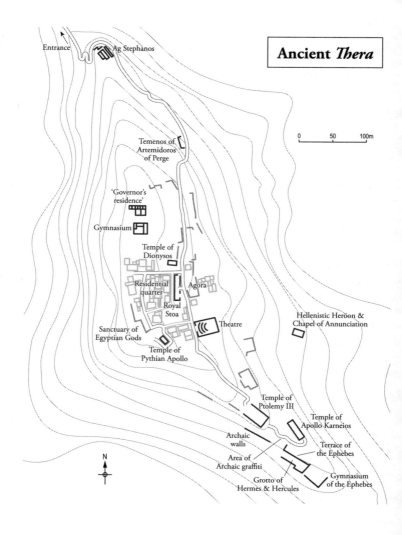

Ancient *Thera*

Entrance

Ag Stephanos

0   50   100m

Temenos of
Artemidoros
of Perge

'Governor's
residence'

Gymnasium

Temple of
Dionysos

Residential
quarter

Agora

Royal
Stoa

Theatre

Hellenistic Heröon &
Chapel of Annunciation

Sanctuary of
Egyptian Gods

Temple of
Pythian Apollo

Temple of
Ptolemy IH

Temple of
Apollo Karneios

Archaic
walls

Terrace of
the Ephebes

Area of
Archaic graffiti

Grotto of
Hermès & Hercules

Gymnasium
of the Ephebes

N

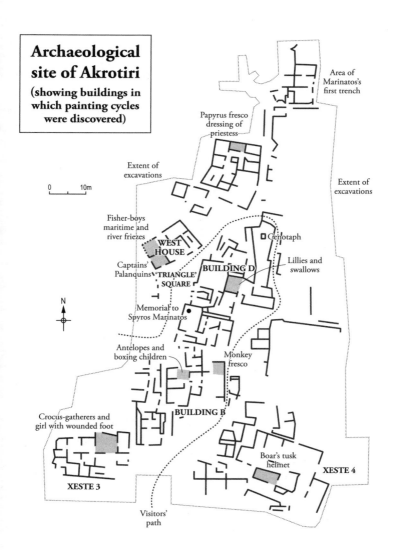

Archaeological site of Akrotiri

(showing buildings in which painting cycles were discovered)

Area of Marinatos's first trench

Papyrus fresco dressing of priestess

Extent of excavations

0   10m

Extent of excavations

Fisher-boys maritime and river friezes

Cenotaph

WEST HOUSE

BUILDING D

Lillies and swallows

Captains' Palanquins

TRIANGLE SQUARE

N

Memorial to Spyros Marinatos

Antelopes and boxing children

Monkey fresco

BUILDING B

Crocus-gatherers and girl with wounded foot

Boar's tusk helmet

XESTE 4

XESTE 3

Visitors' path

Nigel McGilchrist is an art historian who has lived in the Mediterranean—Italy, Greece and Turkey—for over 30 years, working for a period for the Italian Ministry of Arts and then for six years as Director of the Anglo-Italian Institute in Rome. He has taught at the University of Rome, for the University of Massachusetts, and was for seven years Dean of European Studies for a consortium of American universities. He lectures widely in art and archaeology at museums and institutions in Europe and the United States, and lives near Orvieto.